DEDICATION

This Book is dedicated first to My Lord Jesus Christ for giving me a full and abundant life. It is also dedicated to my loving husband and children whose love has made me a better person all around. It is further dedicated to my officers and firemen who every day, put their lives on the line and on hold in service to us all. To Rich Focht for being such as strong and consistent mentor believing I could do it and making me believe I could do it. To Bill Eckleberry for being a friend and mentor. To Mark Repp for letting me help hold a line for the greater good. To James Senay for thinking this might make a good book and pursuing this to this end! Finally to my SC3/IAOCC Chaplains who are living their lives in service to our King every day, you have my deepest and profound love and respect. You have my heart! You are all my heroes!

6/24/15

ABOUT THE AUTHOR

 Dr. Tracy Elder is the founder of the International Alliance of Chaplain Corps and is a local Law Enforcement Chaplain for her community. She is also the Senior Pastor of Set Free Ministries at The Well.

Dr. Tracy Elder is no stranger to Stress and Trauma having spent close to 20 years as a Chaplain and in Disaster Response, which taught her the importance of relevant help bridging the gap between the world and the Church.

Her experience as a Law Enforcement Chaplain and Prison Chaplaincy has equipped and enabled her to rise in her field and help many in crisis.

Dr. Tracy is passionate about training people up to lead and the possibility of healing and wholeness in Christ in whom she has found acceptance, purpose and healing for herself.

Dr, Tracy Elder
PO Box 11
Tiffin, Ohio 44883

DISCLAIMER

This book is a compilation of creative nonfiction. The stories contained within this book may not be entirely factual, as they are based upon the author's life experiences and recollections over the last several decades. All attempts have been made to accurately recount the author's recollections, but the human mind is not perfect. The stories and recollections contained in the book are not written as word-for-word transcripts, but represent a synopsis of the general conversations. The author has done her best to retell the conversations and stories in a way that evokes the feeling and meaning of what was actually said and what actually happened in a hope that others may benefit from the lessons contained in the stories and recollections.

In order to maintain the complete anonymity of all persons involved, the author has changed the names of all individuals and the locations of all events. To protect the privacy of all individuals, victims as well as perpetrators, the author has also changed many of the identifying characteristics including physical descriptions, occupations, and places of residence.

To aid the reader, in some situations, the author has combined several stories and recollections into a new story line to provide greater depth and understanding. The "who" of the stories and recollections are not nearly as important as the lessons to be learned from the "what and why" of the stories and recollections.

TABLE OF CONTENTS

PART 1
A CHAPLAIN'S LIFE

CHAPTER 1

LIFE IS FRAGILE

"Hi, Chaplain Meg? It's Mary at the SO. Are you available to head out to Township Road 151? There has been a suicide. Teenager. Chief wants to know if you can bring a couple of your chaplains and head over there."

"Yeah I can be there in 20. I'll grab two more chaps and head that way. A suicide you say? Any other info?" Meg asked patiently.

"No, that's all I know. They should fill you in when you get there. Will call if something new comes in." said Mary. Meg thought she could hear the weariness in Mary's voice.

Lord, it's so much harder when it's the younglings. Meg thought sadly. She took the teenage suicides personally. She thought back to her own abusive childhood and at how close she had come to running away and/or ending it all. That was not an option now. Then, it was a constant companion from an early age. *Thank you Lord for saving me, even from myself.* She thought. Meg had grabbed Chaplains Leanna and Elaine and headed to the scene.

"Oh wow." Meg said as she drove up to the farm house. There were literally 100 kids on the lawn. "We better be on our toes girls." Meg said under her breath. She and her crew exited the vehicle and immediately the teens surrounded them, asking questions.

Meg put her arms around their shoulders and walked, bobbing her as she listened to them talk. Her other chaplains followed suit. Meg made her way to front of the house.

"I will see if I can get you that information." She said looking at the kids she had been walking with. "I will be right back out in a bit. Before I go in though, can you guys help me out?" The two young men looked at her and nodded. She gave the instructions to go out and spread the word among the rest of the crowd that she was going to get them some answers. She sensed their trepidation. This was a hard one for anyone, but for teenagers it was especially hard. She never knew how they would respond or react. Right now they were doing good though. They were following directions and cooperating. She prayed that it continued.

As soon as the young men left her side she headed into the house. Just inside the door was the living room, filled with personnel. She knew almost all of them at this point. She looked around until she spotted Chief.

"Hey Chief! Wow that's a lot of kids! What do we have?" Meg asked.

"Teenager shot himself in the basement. He was apparently on the phone with his girlfriend and she broke up with him. She had a friend with her while she was on the phone with him. She heard the shot and the screaming and became hysterical and her friend started making phone calls and here we are with a 100 kids trying to hold it together." Chief said as he looked out the window at the sea of teenagers.

"What do you need me to do?" Meg asked looking out the window as well.

"See that barn down to the south? Can you get them to all move down there? We have to move some of the vehicles around on the yard. Sean is coming with the van to take the body and we have to get him in first. Every time we go out there to move the trucks the kids crowd us. We don't want them to leave but we have

to get this done. Go work your mojo and herd them down there."
Chief said pointing to the barn in the distance.

"On it." Meg said, heading to the door.

"Hey Meg…" Chief said before she left. "We'll be waiting for
you to do your thing when you are done out there." Meg nodded.
She knew what he meant. She had been working with her guys
for some time now and they had their own way of dealing with the
hard stuff. She would be ready. "Be back soon." She said quietly
and headed out the door.

Outside, Meg grabbed her Chaplains and explained what was
going on. She asked them to go into the crowd and find at least
2 adults that weren't family members that the kids were gathered
around and to bring them to her. She told them to ask them if
they would be willing to help her, and that it was important.

Meg learned a long time ago that she would rather invite people to participate rather than have to demand that they comply.
It was easier with partnerships and cooperation than it was with
demands. She had learned that the hard way and never wanted to
repeat that mistake.

Her chaplains headed into the crowd as a group of teens came
toward her. She put her arms around their shoulders again and
listened intently to their questions. She answered them and again
asked them to help her by letting the others know that she was going to be making an announcement in the next few minutes. The
teens eagerly headed through the crowd with the update.

Two adults approached Meg from her left. One identified himself as the coach from the local high school and the other was a
family friend. Both were weary, but willing to help in any way. Meg
expressed gratitude for their willingness. She explained the situation and asked them to help her move the kids in the direction
of the barn and their help in keeping them there. She explained
that she would be making an announcement in a few minutes and
if they could get the kids moving now that would work best. She

pointed out the teens she had already dispatched with the same task and they went to work.

Five minutes later, Meg was standing in front of the large crowd of kids and adults making the official announcement that their friend had died of his injuries. She expressed gratitude to all of them for being there for this family, and that their love and concern was truly appreciated. She told them they didn't have to leave but would appreciate it if they would stay down here near the barn as the vehicles were moved and the first responders maneuvered to finish their work here. She answered several questions and then asked them to pray with her for the family. She began with the Lord's Prayer and the kids had their heads bowed and participated in praying too. When she was finished she asked them to hang out and take care of one another as she went back up to the house to do her next task. She would be back out for the family shortly. When Meg reentered the house she found Chief looking out the window at the kids.

"Is that good? Are they far enough back?" Meg asked looking out too.

"Yeah, they're good. How did you get them to move back there?" Chief said still looking out the window.

"Mojo, remember?" Meg said smiling. *It's all you Lord.* She thought to herself. *Thank you for your presence and your wisdom.*

"Are you ready?" Chief asked, still not looking at her. Meg got quiet and still.

"Yep. Are you?" Chief turned around toward the rest of the workers. "Chap comin' through!" He said so everyone could hear. Everything stopped. Everyone inside stood still as Meg followed behind Chief as he made his way through the throng of people and equipment until he reached the basement. Everyone fell in line behind them and followed. Chief stopped a few feet away from where the young man sat against the wall. He was slumped over on his left side a little. Meg could see the open gaping wound in his head where the shotgun had done its damage. It was one of the worst things she had witnessed thus far. The detectives and investigators were still processing the scene but were done with the body for the most part. His hands were bagged after being tested for gunshot residue, which was standard procedure. Nothing else was covered at this point.

Chief looked at Meg and nodded. Meg moved forward to the young man and knelt down, resting her hand on his leg. She could feel the rest of them moving around her kneeling behind and beside her. They all placed a hand on her back or her arms or her head. When she knew they were all there she began to pray. They prayed with her; first the Lord's Prayer in unison, and then in agreement as she prayed that the Lord would comfort this family with His perfect comfort and perfect peace. She prayed that He would be there for each of her guys in the aftermath of this as well. This is too big for us. This is too hard to understand but that He would bring understanding in time and comfort now. When she had finished they all stood in unison and wiped their tears and went back to work. They had to finish it now.

"Sean is ready for him." Chief said. "We will have him bagged up in five. You wanna go get the family now?"

"On it." Meg said, heading up the stairs. "Chief, can I ask something? Can we have Sean wait at the end of the driveway and let the kids have a moment? They have been so good and they have earned it. Can we give them the time to say goodbye here?"

"Anything you want Meg. I'll let Sean know that you are coming and what you want."

"Thanks Chief. I think these kids need this." She met Sean near the top of the stairs.

"Thanks Meg. That prayer thing is always appreciated. I'm glad you're here with us. " Sean said smiling down at her. "It means a lot. So I'm going to bring him up and get him bundled up and get him ready for transport. You are getting the family now right?

Then you want me to wait at the end of the drive for the kids to come by?"

"If it's not too much trouble, yeah. They have been so patient and so good. Do you have time?" Meg asked.

"We can do it. No problem." Sean said smiling. Meg smiled back and squeezed his hand and headed out the door to the crowd.

"Hey everyone. Can I have your attention?" Meg said using her authority voice. The crowd gathered close to her so they could hear what she was saying.

"You guys have been great. I need to bring the family in now so while I'm doing that will you guys pray and help each other out here? I will be back soon." Meg gathered the family from the crowd and escorted them into the house. The mom looked like she was in another world. The father's hands were soaked with blood from trying to revive his son. They had run to him when they heard the shot. The other children were crying and scared and grief-stricken, but walked with their parents toward the house.

Once inside, Meg escorted them to the gurney waiting by the side door where their son was completely zipped inside a body bag and covered with a blanket. Meg's people continued to work out of sight. They were rarely present for this part. They watched from afar sometimes, but rarely interacted at this point. The mom began to rub her son's arm through the layers. She was crying quietly.

"Oh baby, why?" She said over and over. The dad stood on the other side of his son with his hands gripping his own hair breathing harshly.

"I couldn't save him! I couldn't save him. I tried to save him."

The children were holding onto each other and their mother and were crying. They couldn't look at the bag, but had their faces buried in their hands or their mother's back. Meg let her own tears flow. She was feeling it too. She waited a few minutes and then spoke.

"If you would like to pray we can do that now." She said quietly. The mom nodded her head and began to pray over her son. Meg stood quietly as the family took control of the final moments with their son. When it came time for her to close she prayed simply and quietly for God to continue to comfort and grant them peace. And it was done.

Meg escorted the family back into the living room and seated them while Sean and one of the EMT's rolled the gurney outside to the waiting van. Sean drove the van to the end of the driveway and waited for Meg to make the announcement. Meg again addressed the crowd of teens.

"Thank you again for being here. You have been of great comfort to this family and you are so appreciated! We wanted to give you a moment to say goodbye if you want to. You see that van over there? Your friend is in there and the driver is waiting to give you that moment. If you want to you can go over there and put your hand on the van or pray or whatever you need to do just don't open the doors. If you could get in line or go together we are going to wait for you so that everyone has an opportunity. You can go over there right now." Meg said. She had such compassion for these younglings. They were doing so good. They formed a line and quietly and quickly made their way to the van. Some put their hand on the glass and said something. Some put their head against the glass and prayed. Some held hands and sang a song together. Their moment of grief and mourning and togetherness was truly moving.

When the last one had moved away, Meg let Sean know it was good to go. She had seen the tears on his cheeks and reached in to squeeze his hand on the wheel. He squeezed hers back looking straight ahead. He pulled away slowly as if not wanting to leave them. Meg faced the crowd one last time.

"I want you to know that no one has to be alone right now. The coach has opened the school and we have sent over food and drinks. We think it's a good idea for you to go there together. Does anyone need a ride? There are some of you here who can give them a ride right? It's already been tragic tonight so we need you to take care of each other and get there safely and spend some time together. There are some counselors there too in case you need to talk. There's nothing more you can do here tonight but the family is grateful for your love. Will you pray with me one last time tonight and will you take care of each other?"

Meg prayed. Afterward the kids very orderly made their way to their cars and very carefully made their way to the school where counselors were waiting to receive them. In the aftermath, Meg and her chaplains were so grateful that not another single suicide resulted proximate to this incident. Usually with teen suicide they come in clusters. Not this time, thank God.

CHAPTER 2

MANDY

"Hey Chap it's Ellen from Dispatch. Detective James would like you to meet him at the scene of the shooting out on County Road 6. You need the address or did you catch the radio traffic?"

"No I got the address. I will grab another Chaplain and head out there. Will call in when I'm enroute. Thanks Ellen. I hope the rest of your night is quieter!" Meg said.

Meg called Leanna to go with her, one of the many Chaplains she had trained over the past four years. By now had left the Pastorate completely and was doing Chaplaincy full time. Meg had taken all of her Chaplains with her on calls so that they can gain understanding and experience and build relationships within the community and departments. She had founded and built a Chaplain Corps four years ago, which had now become a movement for mobilizing the laity into service in every area of trauma and heartbreak one could imagine. This was going to be one of those calls.

She reminded herself and her Chaplains frequently that Jesus was known as "the man of sorrows acquainted with grief" and they as His people endeavoring to be like Him would eventually become a people of sorrows acquainted with grief. Boy, were they now!

Meg picked up Leanna at her home and then called in to let Ellen in Dispatch know they were on their way. She used the phone instead of the radio so no one in Scanner land would hear that the Chaplain had been dispatched to the scene.

"Do you know any more? It's a shooting right?" Leanna asked.

"That's all I know other than that it's a nineteen-year-old male. I don't know if it's a death notification or a comfort-after-the-fact call," Meg explained.

When they arrived at the house, they entered through the main door. Two women sat on the couch, one in her sixties and one who appeared to be in her forties. The older woman gripped the edge of her seat, knuckles white, elbows on her knees and legs shaking up and down. She looked straight ahead. Her face was a mask of angst and anger, her mouth a harsh, unapproachable slit.

The other woman seemed exhausted and emotionally spent. She was slumped on the couch with her head buried in her hands, moaning. Meg had never heard that sound but she knew instinctively that it was the deep sound of grief and mourning. It was almost guttural from the very essence of her soul.

"I might be the same way under the right circumstances; add the right kind of stress and pressure and we are all capable of anything." Meg thought. Detective James motioned for to Meg to join him in a room off to her left. She moved silently past the two women and entered the room.

Meg had always liked Detective James. He had always been friendly, compassionate and thorough. He cared deeply about others. He had great communication skills when talking with both victims and alleged perpetrators. His work ethic was incredible and he never cut corners. He was former military and his manner showed it.

"Hey Meg. Thanks for coming out. Leanna, you too. Did you get briefed on what we have?" Detective James asked.

"No just that there was a shooting and the victim was a nineteen-year-old male." Meg replied.

She began to look around the room as the Detective filled her in on what she needed to know and what he needed her to do. She observed bandage wrappers and tubing left behind by the EMT's who had worked on the young man. She noted blood and other biological matter spattered about the room. She could see traces of bone and hair, too.

Detective James explained that the victim, Ronnie Newall, had been in the room with some friends when he was shot in the back of the head. They were still in the early stages of investigation, and piecing things together. The friends had been transported back to the SO to be questioned and he had the gun in evidence. He stated that Ronnie had been transported to St. Patrick's Hospital over an hour ago in critical condition. He was alive at the time of transport.

"Those two women out there are his Grandmother, Mandy and His Aunt, Lois. Grandma isn't happy with us and doesn't want to talk. I need you to transport them up to St. Pat's and give me an update on his condition. They are the next of kin as far as I know. Like I said, she doesn't want to talk to us. She's pretty hard. I don't know that I wouldn't be too if it were me. I still have a few hours ahead of me here so call when you get word on his condition. If you need anything just call too. Again thanks Meg. It's appreciated."

"Anything I can do, Detective. You have the harder job. I appreciate you more than you will ever know." Meg said.

Meg and Leanna went back out into the living room where the two women were still seated in exactly the same positions they had been in when Meg entered the house.

"Mandy, I'm Chaplain Meg Redle with the County Sheriff's Office." Meg began.

"What the hell do you want?!" Mandy shouted.

"Hey. I'm transportation. The detective called me to take you and your daughter to the hospital if you want to go." Meg said with her hands up. "So if you're ready, I have a car waiting outside."

Mandy was up off the couch like a shot and had her coat and boots on and was waiting by the door impatiently while Meg and Leanna helped Lois up off the couch and into her coat.

That's not normal. Meg thought of Mandy's behavior. *There must be something more...*

Meg and Leanna led the two women to the car and got them settled into the back seat. It had been a cold, windy, rainy, miserable day and it looked like it wasn't going to get any better any time soon. She started the long drive to St. Pat's.

Meg watched Mandy from the rearview mirror observing her demeanor. She was staring out the window, stock still. Her mouth was set in a thin, grim line. Lois moaned and slumped against the seat, all strength sapped from her.

"It's just like her all over again!" Lois wailed. "It's just like her!"

Mandy's head whipped around and the look of rage and disgust was aimed directly at Lois.

"Shut up! Shut up! Don't you talk about it! Don't you say it again! Don't you talk about Her!' She said in a menacing voice. She whipped her head back towards the window again and stared.

Wow! Meg thought. There is *definitely* more here.

"Mandy, does Ronnie's mom or dad need to be called? Do they live out of state or something? We can call and get them headed this way if you want or if there is someone else we need to call for you we can do that now." Meg said in a calm voice.

Nothing about Mandy's demeanor changed at all. She didn't move, she stared out the window never acknowledging Meg or her question.

"...cause we have some time before we get there and we would be able to get them heading this way so we can meet them up there..." Meg said quietly.

Mandy's head snapped up and met Meg's gaze in the rearview mirror.

"His mother's dead and his father's in prison! There's no one else to call, ok, there's just me! There's just me!" Mandy spat out venemously. She then turned her head back to the window and stared one more, out past the horizon and into nothingness.

It's going to be a long ride. Meg thought.

A little over an hour later, Meg pulled into the parking lot of St. Pat's Hospital and pulled into a spot where the emergency vehicles parked. Meg opened the door for Mandy to exit the rear of the vehicle and went around the other side to help Leanna with Lois. Mandy was standing by the entrance door tapping her foot impatiently as Meg and Leanna slowly helped Lois along. The poor woman had no strength left!

Meg led the ladies to a waiting room and left Leanna with them so she could take care of them while Meg got information. Meg was directed to the trauma unit and found the Doctor she needed to speak with.

"Dr. Cho, I'm Chaplain Meg with the County Sheriff's Office." She said showing her ID. "I have the next of kin for Ronnie Newall. Can you update me on his condition?"

"Great, are they in the waiting room? I have paperwork for them. Can you see if they are willing to sign the organ donor forms?" he said handing her a clipboard.

"So...he's dead?" Meg asked.

"We have him on machines keeping blood flowing to his organs. He had registered as an organ donor and we have matches. We prefer the next of kin to sign too. The bullet entered his brain here," he said placing his hand on the area of his head right below and behind his right ear.

"The bullet is still lodged in the skull, but it caused significant damage to his brain and there are no signs of brain activity or of life. When we turn off the machines he will stop breathing."

"Can I see him now before I bring in his family?" Meg asked. "I would prefer to tell them before we talk about the paperwork. I'm not familiar with your forms so if you let me inform her of the facts then you can reaffirm it with her and talk to her about the paperwork. We should approach her straightforwardly. She seems pretty shaken up right now, and showing some signs of aggression. There's clearly more in the pot than I'm aware of, but I think we should cross one bridge at a time. Let's see how it goes."

Dr. Cho escorted Meg to Ronnie's room. Meg took note of his condition, the machines, the tubes, the monitors and the bloody bandage on the back of his head. She asked questions about the bandage; could it be changed before she brought the family in, only to find out that it had been changed ten to fifteen minutes before; there was so much blood loss that each bandage had scarcely been added before it needed to be replaced. It would be soaked through by the time she brought them in anyway. She asked about the heart monitors, the respirator and the tubes. When she had the information she felt she needed she asked the Doctor if he was ready.

Chaplain Meg and Dr. Cho made their way to the waiting room. Dr. Cho waited just outside the door speaking with the nurses about preparation after the next of kin signed off while Meg told Mandy of Ronnie's condition.

"Mandy, Lois I need to speak with you for a minute so I need to know that you are hearing me. I need to tell about Ronnie's condition. Are you with me?" Meg said.

"I'm not a child just tell me!" Mandy said roughly.

"Dr. Cho is right outside and he will speak with you as well. I have seen Ronnie too, myself. Mandy, Lois, I'm sorry but they are telling me that Ronnie is brain dead." Meg waited for a reaction. Lois shook her head and slumped over her knees, crying softly. Mandy didn't flinch, didn't move at all; just stared at Meg menacingly.

"Mandy do you understand what I'm telling you, hon? They are saying that Ronnie is brain dead. He is on machines to keep his blood flowing to his organs because he was a registered organ donor." Meg said backing to the door and beckoning in Dr. Cho. "Dr. Cho wants to speak with you concerning Ronnie's injury and the organ donation permission." Meg said as she introduced Dr. Cho.

Dr. Cho began to talk to Mandy about the specific injuries to Ronnie's brain, the lack of brain activity and of options. Ronnie's life had ended when the bullet entered his brain. Mandy listened intently but gave no response or reaction. Dr. Cho started to talk to her about the forms and she turned away.

"Why don't we go see him first Dr. Cho. Mandy would you like to see Ronnie now?" Meg said looking directly at Dr. Cho. Mandy was off the couch like a shot again.

"Before we see him there are a few things you need to know. Ronnie is lying in the bed and his eyes are closed. He looks like he's sleeping. There are tubes in his arms and nose and a respirator has been inserted to keep oxygen flowing to his organs. He is not able to breathe on his own. There are monitors and you can see he has a heartbeat and they are monitoring it and his blood pressure. There is another monitor with a running flat line and that is what indicates the lack of brain activity. He has a bandage on the back of his head right below his right ear and you will see blood and other matter on it. It is covering the open wound which is still seeping. You can touch him but don't remove anything from him. Ok? Mandy do you understand what I'm telling you?"

Mandy looked pale. It was the time her demeanor had changed even an iota since Meg had laid eyes on her.

"Do you have any questions?" Meg asked patiently.

"No." Mandy responded hoarsely.

Meg had made the mistake before of not preparing family for what they could expect to see when viewing their loved one at a scene, as opposed to a funeral home. Out here it is still raw and full force while at the funeral home they are cleaned up and posed. It's very disconcerting for families to see their loved one right after death. She had learned that the hard way.

Meg said a silent prayer. She could feel the Lord with her. He understood better than anyone what this was like for Mandy. Father God understood what it was like to lose a son to violence and the grief of it. He also understood the joy of receiving His son back to Himself in reunion. Meg sincerely hoped that was possible here for Mandy too.

"Ok. If you are ready then follow me." Meg said, opening the door.

Dr. Cho had expressed to Meg that there was little time left for the organs to be harvested and viable. He had pronounced Ronnie brain dead more than two hours before. There were people matched and waiting, so Meg was cognizant of the time.

She escorted Mandy and Lois to Ronnie's room bringing her a chair so she could sit beside him. Leanna brought a chair over the Lois as well. Mandy sat beside Ronnie and rubbed his arm gently. She looked at him so intently as if willing him to respond to her.

"Ronnie, wake up! Ronnie if you hear me, wake up! Show them you are still here!" She said. The pain in her voice was so tangible that everyone could feel her desperation.

At her words, everyone including Meg lowered their eyes as tears tugged them downwards. Some staff members moved away or went out of the room. Meg looked out the door and met Dr. Cho's gaze. His eyes told her that time was up.

"You're all I have left of her." Mandy said quietly as she continued to rub his arm. Nothing changed on any of the monitors there was no response.

"Mandy..." Meg said quietly, "I need to speak with you. It's important. Can I talk to you in the hallway? We won't go far. You can still see him from here."

Mandy jumped up from the chair and whisked herself into the hallway, turning on Meg with a look so full of anger and grief and said in a low, menacing tone, "What the hell do you have to say to me? What do you want from me that is so important? Just say it!" Mandy growled. She was staring at Ronnie as she stood there with Meg.

"Mandy, I need to tell you how wonderful I think your grandson is." Meg said looking directly at Mandy.

Mandy looked at Meg with an "are you seriously kidding me right now!" look, most likely trailing a few expletives. She said nothing, but turned her head back to see Ronnie.

"Mandy, I know that your grandson is wonderful because he, at some point in his young life, made a decision that if he were ever in this situation he wanted to help others to live, if possible. That is a testimony to how you raised him. He thought of others, Mandy. I can't think of anything more wonderful from a young man. I'm so sorry you are in this position, and it's not ok. He should be home listening to music or out on a date or something. But he's not, he's here and it's not ok. Mandy, the Doctor needs a decision. I will tell them whatever you want me to. If you say no then I will tell them that but if you want to consider Ronnie's wishes then I will have Dr. Cho explain it. I'm so sorry but we are out of time. What do you want me to do?" Meg's heart was breaking as she watched a single tear fall down Mandy's cheek.

Mandy's lips were quivering as she said the words, "Get me the damn papers!"

"Yes ma'am." Meg said and she touched her arm as she turned to get the Doctor. Mandy and the Doctor talked for several minutes as Meg looked on.

This is too tragic. She thought. *That is too much for one person to lose. I don't know how she manages it, Lord. I know you love her and want to comfort her but I am not sure what to say in the wake of the enormity of her losses.*

Meg watched as Mandy signed the papers the Doctor present-ed. She could see the anguish and the pain etched in Mandy's fea-tures. She looked frail and defeated, but defiant at the same time. Meg moved toward them as they arose from the couch.

"My team is waiting, so I have to go get prepped. Mandy, I'm so sorry for your loss, but I am grateful for the opportunity to help others live. Again, I'm sorry."

"Can we have 5 more minutes with him?" Meg asked the Doctor.

He nodded. "Yes but we have to move quickly now." His eyes told her that he had transitioned into work mode now and was fo-cused on the task ahead.

"Mandy, I'm sorry honey but it's time to say goodbye for now. Are you ready to go back in?" Meg asked quietly.

Mandy didn't say anything; she just started walking toward Ronnie's room. Her shoulders were slumped and her head was down. She looked so exhausted. Meg followed along behind her in silence. She had learned a long time ago that if you can't improve on silence, don't try. Sometimes there just aren't words.

Mandy sat next to Ronnie and began to rub his arm. She was so tender and gentle now. Before, in desperation, she had been rougher trying to get him to react.

"I love you Ronnie. You were all I had left of her. Tell your mother that I still remember her and that I love her. Tell your brother that I love him too. Sleep now. Grandma's gotta go home now." Mandy ended her words in a sob. She stood shakily to her feet and put her hand on his cheek and kissed his forehead. She looked down on him one last time with such love and adoration that Meg's eyes welled with tears.

Lord, give me something for her! Meg begged inside herself. She so desperately wanted to comfort this woman. Mandy straightened herself and grabbed her coat from the rack, walking with purpose out of the room and towards the parking garage. Meg and Leanna helped Lois get her coat and headed for the car.

"It's going to be a long ride home." Lois said.

The drive home was made in silence. All four women were utterly spent. What was there to say anyway? Now it was time to mourn, and there was no right way or wrong way, there was just their own way. Grief is very personal and everyone does it so differently. Meg's role would be whatever Mandy would let her be.

As Meg pulled the car in to the driveway she noticed that the Detectives were gone, but that there was an angry looking man pacing in the driveway and the front door was open on the house.

"Mandy, do you know this man?" Meg asked concerned.

"It's my landlord." Mandy said with ire.

Mandy exited the back of the vehicle the same time Meg exited the front.

"Who's going to pay for this? I'm not paying for this! Who's gonna clean this up? I'm not doing it! What the hell happened here?" The man shouted.

Mandy was ready for a fight. All the tension, all the anger now had a target. He had put himself in the line of fire and she was willing to light it up.

"Woah, woah!" Meg said getting in between them. "I am. I am going to clean it up and it won't cost you anything. I am. You can inspect it when I'm done so you are satisfied. We do this. If you want a professional afterward we can help arrange it but for now I will do it." Mandy and the man stopped moving and stared at her.

"I have everything in my vehicle. I am ready to get started I just need to help get Mandy and Lois settled inside. I have already seen the room and I have everything we need to clean it for biohazard and it will take about three hours. I promise we will do a good job. Are you ok with that, sir?" Meg asked.

"It better be done right!" he said. "I'll be back in three hours."

"Thank you." Meg said.

Mandy stared at Meg for at least a minute with emotions warring on her face and then silently walked into the house and took her position on the couch. Meg and Leanna silently got the gear they needed to clean the room. They walked past Mandy and Lois without a word, and locked themselves in Ronnie's room.

Over the next 2 ½ hours the Chaplains worked tirelessly and meticulously removing the blood, brain matter, skin, bone and other matter from every crevice of the dresser and corner of the room. They checked and rechecked to make sure they had not missed anything. They worked in silence for the most part. It was a somber and gruesome task. It was also a labor of love. Meg couldn't stand the thought of Mandy or Lois having to deal with this, let alone under the pressure of the landlord. The compassion that both women felt for this family was profound. This family had lost too much and this was a small comfort that could be given. It was the comfort of knowing that it was done and resolved and not a task to face or fear.

"We can give them this, Lord. Thank you for the opportunity to serve and in one small area maybe bring peace of mind." Meg thought. It might be the only peace they could offer that meant anything. It wasn't empty words, it was love in action. Jesus was the example here still. He would have washed her feet.

When they had finally finished and the Landlord had approved, Meg and Leanna gathered up all of the materials and packed them in the trunk of the car. Meg walked back into the house one last time.

"Mandy," she said as she slid her card across the coffee table in front of Mandy, "We are going now. The landlord shouldn't bother you over the cleaning. He signed off that he accepted the work as complete and satisfactory. Here's my card if you have any questions or concerns about anything. If you need help with the funeral my cell phone number is on there too and it's 24 hours if you need anything. Call for any reason."

Mandy never moved or made eye contact. She just sat there staring straight ahead. Meg left the card and said goodbye to Lois and went out the door praying silently for the ladies and for herself.

Meg sat in her office filing the routine paperwork, desk stained with coffee rings and old, forgotten pieces of paper.

"Chaplain Meg! There's a really scary woman out here!" Rose said under her breath.

"Who is it Rose? Did she give a name?" Meg asked, amused. She loved Rose, all four foot tall 75 years of her!

"No, she just said she needed to see you and stared at me when I asked any questions. I mean she **stared through** me like I was a door or something. She's a tough cookie I can tell. Shall I send her back?" Rose said breathlessly.

"Sure, hon, send her back." Meg said smiling calmly. Meg rose from her desk as the woman entered her office. She looked familiar. Meg was in shock when she realized that it was Mandy, the grandmother from the shooting four months ago. She hadn't heard anything from her since Meg and Leanna had attended Ronnie's viewing at the Funeral Home.

"Mandy?" Meg asked moving toward her. "Well hello! It's good to see you. How are you doing?" Mandy shook Meg's outstretched hand and sat in the chair Meg motioned her to. Meg sat down across from her offering her a bottled water. Meg took the bottle automatically and twisted it around in her hands anxiously. She was nervous and fidgety.

"I just thought you should know..." Mandy said standing up. She began to pace the room, avoiding any eye contact with Meg. Meg could see that her hands were shaking.

"Know what, hon? I'm here for you." Meg said quietly.

Mandy's back was to Meg as she began to speak again. "It's because you cleaned it up... because you and Leanna cleaned it up. I just thought you should know." She was faltering. Her hands dropped to her sides and her head hung down below her shoulders. Meg was patient and didn't push. She waited. Finally she stood and walked over to Mandy and stood just behind her.

"Take a drink Mandy. We have all the time in the world. I'm listening."

Mandy's hands shook as she tried to remove the Chief from the bottled water. Meg reached over and covered Mandy's hands with her own, opening the bottle. Mandy turned and looked Meg square in the eyes. Meg took a step forward and speaking only with her own eyes embraced Mandy in an all-consuming, accepting hug.

At first Mandy stiffened at the contact, and then gave into it. She hugged Meg back with a fierceness that made Meg feel such compassion for the older woman. Meg silently prayed that Mandy would find Him in all of this and that He would give her the words of comfort that He had for Mandy that would help her start to heal. None would come without Him. Meg let go of the embrace and led Mandy back to the chair.

"What do you think I should know Mandy?" Meg asked quietly.

"Ronnie's mother was my daughter. His father was her drug dealer and her pimp." Mandy said looking at Meg with steel in her face as if daring Meg to react. Meg nodded in understanding as she waited for Mandy to begin again.

Mandy was straight and stiff as she continued, as if ensconced in armor.

"Ronnie was five years old. He was in school the day his father murdered my daughter and their infant son. He shot her in the face and chest and shot that baby boy. He left them in that field to rot. It was three or four days before anyone found them. The baby was so decomposed that I never got to see him; he was only three months old. It was closed caskets for both of them." Mandy said, looking away and taking a drink of the water. She stood again and started pacing. Meg sat waiting patiently.

"When she died, I went to the church to get her buried Christian. The first one I went to said that my daughter was in hell but that I could be saved." She said it with such venom but Meg sensed the deeper pain underneath. This woman had loved her daughter deeply.

"I went to another church and they said I could rent the hall for $750.00 which included the Pastor's fee. Do I look like I have that kind of money? My daughter didn't have any insurance or estate to sign over to anyone either and boy did they ask the financial questions! I went to another one and they flat out said no because we weren't members. So the funeral director did it. We had it all at the funeral home. I know what my daughter was! But she was my daughter and I loved her. They treated her like she was some kind of trash. But that baby... that baby didn't do anything to anyone and he deserved better than that! He should have been buried Christian!" Mandy said spitting out the words that Meg was sure tasted bitter. "So when Ronnie died I didn't even try to go to a church. I had the same funeral director do it. I know you said you could help with the funeral but I didn't want any of you people after that because they made it plain that there is no God for people like us." Meg shook her head knowingly. She knew that what Mandy had experienced was real...and wrong. Mandy continued before Meg could respond.

"Her murderer was arrested and the trial was a nightmare. I had to sit and listen to that SOB's lawyer talk like my daughter deserved what he did. Like she was to blame! I heard for months and years now my daughter being called a "Crack Whore" and how if you live like that you shouldn't be surprised that she died like that. She had her reasons and I couldn't save her. Her father ran off after I found out that he had been messing with her. She was six. I caught him in the act. That SOB blamed her for it then. I tried to get her help but I couldn't afford it. I didn't get child support or nothing from him. I had to work two jobs to support my girls. I did the best I could. I couldn't save her." Mandy said crying now.

Meg stiffened as a flood of memories from her own trauma surfaced and made themselves known. "No," she thought, "you won't rob me of the chance to set a captive free as I am free." She thought as she relaxed and focused on Mandy again.

"Every year now I have to go before that parole board and tell them why that SOB needs to stay in prison! What a no brainer! He murdered my baby and their infant - his own son! It's never over for me! Every time it comes around it's brought back up in the paper again and it drags up old memories, and I have to relive it all. He don't care. It ain't costing him nothing. He gets out of his cell once a year for the show!"

Mandy sat down in the chair, her eyes flashing with anger and pain. She stared at Meg as if daring her to challenge her experience or tell her is wasn't so or to justify. Meg held Mandy's gaze hoping she could see the acceptance in her eyes. Finally Meg spoke.

"Mandy, I need to tell you something and I need you to hear what I am saying so I need to look at me while I tell you." Her voice was steady and serious. *Lord, give me the right words, the healing words, the redeeming words. Meg prayed silently. She needs to know the real you. It's the only way she will find peace. Help me help her Lord.*

Meg leaned forward and placed her elbows on her knees, clasping her hands together. She looked Mandy directly in the eyes and said, "Mandy, hear what I'm saying to you. Mandy, I'm sorry for what my brethren have done to you. You're right. Your daughter and grandson didn't deserve that. You didn't deserve that. Mandy, I didn't know you then but if I had been there, if I had known, Mandy I would've taken care of your daughter and your grandson and I would've taken care of you. Mandy I'm sorry. I'm here now. What can I do? What do you need?" Tears were flowing down Meg's cheeks as compassion flowed from her. She grieved for Mandy. She understood all too well how outsiders were treated. Mandy didn't know the Jesus that they showed her was one wrought by men and their rules. She intended to show her the true Jesus from His own words and by His spirit if Mandy would give her at shot at sharing at some point. Mandy's lip began to quiver and Meg watched as Mandy's countenance melted in front of her.

"I think I need to talk to someone. I think I have to. The thoughts, the nightmares, I can't live like this anymore!" Mandy said as she began to cry.

"That I can do. Let me make a phone call." Meg said. Meg called Leanna and got the two of them together and Mandy began grief counseling. Six weeks later Mandy was a different woman. She was finally on her way to healing. In her counseling with Leanna, Mandy found the true Jesus, the one who would never leave her nor forsake her. For the first time in years Mandy was not only alive, but she was living.

"Chaplain Meg, Mandy's here!" Rose announced, beaming at the woman behind her.

"Mandy! It's so good to see you honey!" Meg said, moving in for a hug.

"You too, Meg." Mandy said hugging her back.

Meg looked at Mandy and saw the concern creasing her eyebrows.

"What is it Mandy? Is it parole time again? Gosh, it has been at least five months since you were in last. You look so good but I can see the worry on your face. I'm here for you. Whatever it is." Meg said, remembering the months of counseling leading to forgiveness and faith and freedom to live for Mandy. She was reminded of her own journey of freedom as well. Mandy's had paralleled her own in so many ways. It was God that made the difference in both of their walks. God is good!

Mandy reached into her purse and pulled out a packet of papers. There were at least a half dozen letters she handed to Meg. Meg could see Mandy's hand shake as she held the papers out to her.

"What are these?" Meg asked.

"Just read them. I can't explain." Mandy said flustered.

"Ok." Meg replied and opened the first paper.

The papers were letters written by people who had received Ronnie's organs. They were filled with testimonies of gratitude and hope, humility and desire to serve others. They mourned with her for the sacrifice. They acknowledged the ugly fact that one died so they could live, compelling them to live their lives in the light of responsibility and weight. They had a chance to live now that one life had ended.

Meg had never considered that before, how the recipients might feel. It never occurred to her that there might be a contemplative groundedness that came with receiving life from the death of another; that there was a weight to it.

"Mandy these are wonderful! What concerns you? What has you spooked?" Meg asked. Mandy filtered through the letters and pulled out a large envelope. "Here read this one." She said handing the letter to Meg.

Meg opened the coarse paper and found finger painting obviously made by a child. The painting was of a family scene. There was a house, trees and birds. Four stick figures stood in a group under some leafy trees. Obviously the little girl who was featured prominently in the scene was the recipient of organs. Primary colors of green, blue, red and yellow were used to paint the picture.

"Mandy, this is beautiful but I still don't understand. What are you worried about?" Meg asked confused.

"They want to meet me!!" Mandy said forcefully.

"And that's scary why?" Meg asked.

"That one that you're holding. That little girl. She received Ronnie's Corneas. Oh Meg! If I look into her eyes...will I see him?" Mandy asked with a hitch in her voice.

"Oh Mandy, I don't know." Meg said her eyes wide with wonder herself. "What I do know is this; if you want to meet with them, we will be with you. Why don't you let us work out some of the details? We can put together a party in the park and if you decide you want to meet them then you come. If you decide you can't then we will meet with them for you. What do you think?" Meg asked excited.

"I'm willing. I'm willing. Ok." Mandy said nodding her head. "Let's do it."

Meg and her chaplains went to work and made the arrangements. They were ready when the big day arrived. There was cake and balloons and barbecue in the park. The sky was cloudless and sun warmed the grass and the people relaxing on it.

Meg had spent time praying and contemplating the question that Mandy had asked. She had come to the conclusion that God had something planned that would bring Mandy into a greater joy and peace with all of this. It was bound to be a bittersweet moment in her heart. A reminder of all she had lost, true, but God has been with her and had made her stronger. This would be a test of endurance as well as where she was with Him and where He was leading her forward. Meg prayed that the memories of her grandson would be a comfort to her now and not just an open gaping wound. God was still mending her wounds. Healing wasn't complete yet. So Meg continued to pray.

One by one they came. The first to arrive was a young man about 22. Meg watched both Mandy and the young man for their reactions. Mandy seemed to be holding her own for now. She was nervous but seemed alright. Meg was glad that Mandy had decided to come and see the life from her loss. She knew this was going to be difficult to say the least, but hoped that in so many ways it would bring healing.

The young man walked confidently down the hill and made his way directly to where Mandy sat in the shade. The young man was smiling down at Mandy and as she started to get up he took her hands in his and kneelt down in front of her on one knee. He looked like he was proposing! Meg stared in awe as he began to speak.

"I am so glad to finally meet you. I'm Mitch. I received Ronnie's liver. Words can't express how grateful I am for the gift of life I have been given and the grief I feel for you for your loss. I'm a poor substitute for your grandson but I am here to make you a vow." He said looking her directly in the eye. "I vow that I will live worthy of the gift. I have been given the chance to live a life denied to your grandson. I vow that I will take care of myself and honor his memory by helping others and paying it forward. I vow to be a good man to the best of my ability. I vow to always remember what it cost you so that I can live. This is a symbol of my vow." He said removing his hands from hers where he had placed a medal. "I just finished a half marathon. I am a runner. It's the first one I have been able to enter in 2 years. I ran for Ronnie and for you as well as me. I finished in the middle and it was hard but it was fun. I felt alive!" he said with tears welling in his eyes. "I promise to live worthy of the gift." He said standing. He leaned in and kissed Mandy's cheek.

Mandy put her hand on his cheek and the emotion on her face told the tale. Tears were running down her face and she was unable to speak. She looked at him and nodded with a smile. It was a bittersweet smile, a shy smile, but it was full of pride and hope and love.

Meg and her chaplains watched the exchange and felt incredibly moved. There wasn't a dry eye among them. It was simply beautiful. Meg was so grateful for this opportunity to see something good come out of the tragic circumstances, to see Mandy find peace.

Thank you Lord. This wouldn't be possible without you. It is you alone who can restore a broken and battered life. It is in you alone that there is hope and redemption. You alone can take us from the ashes and reconcile the pain and mourning and use it to heal and bring others to you. You are still good, still in control and still moving us toward an intended end with good in it. I love you. I want you know it, that with everything that is within me I love you Lord. Meg thought to herself.

The other recipients filtered in in a steady trickle. There was a young man who had received a Kidney. He was fun! He stood beside Mandy as she sat in the chair while his wife took pictures. He had his back to the camera and his arm around Mandy as he lifted his shirt to show his scar for the picture. He smiled wide, beaming at his wife as she snapped pictures. He was definitely working it. Everyone was laughing as he modeled and mugged for the cameras.

"Give her a hug, George!" his wife Susan said as she continued to take pictures.

"I can do better than that!" he said wrapping Mandy in a hug and kissing her cheek.

Mandy was playing it up too. She was filled with delight and her smile could rival the sun. Meg was giddy with all of the banter. She had taken pictures as well and was struck by what it looked like. To the outside world looking at the scene what would they see? Would they recognize the significance of what was going on here? Would any onlooker know or sense that these were perfect strangers brought together under the most tragic of circumstances? Would anyone outside of this group know what price had been paid to form these relationships? What does it look like? As Meg scrolled through the pictures on her camera she realized that it looked like a family reunion or a birthday celebration. *Yes that's it…it's a celebration.* She thought smiling.

"Here comes the last one!" Leanna said, pointing up the hill.

Meg turned to see the last guest arriving. It was her, Erica, the little girl, the one who had received Ronnie's corneas. She was beautiful! She had long dark curly hair that bounced as she ran down the hill toward them. Her red and white polka dotted dress bobbed up and down as she flew in their direction. She had papers in her hand that flew like a kite behind her as she sped down the hill. She made a beeline straight to Mandy and to everyone's delight she jumped in her lap.

"Are you my grandma Mandy?" Erica asked not waiting for an answer as she gave her the papers. They were more pictures of her family that she had painted. The little girl's head bobbed as she talk nonstop. "This is my dog and this is my sister. I didn't paint my goldfish because I didn't have any gold..."

Meg watched as Mandy looked intently at Erica who was happily telling her everything about her painting. Mandy's head moved as Erica's did. Meg knew that Mandy was trying to look at the girl's eyes. She remembered the question that prompted this gathering. Would Mandy see Ronnie in this girl's eyes? Meg watched carefully as the two interacted. Mandy finally honed in and got very still. Erica was still talking nonstop but was looking directly at Mandy now. As Meg watched she saw Mandy's expression change. At first she looked determined as she searched out the girl's eyes. When she finally locked her gaze onto Erica's she saw her searching intently. She watched as Mandy's expression changed over to wonder and finally to something else as she relaxed. Mandy looked over at Meg with a peaceful, serene gaze nodding and smiling. Meg never asked and Mandy never told her what she saw in Erica's eyes. Meg just accepted that whatever she found there gave Mandy peace, and that was enough.

She had amassed many of those experiences now. She had been working as a Chaplain for more than twenty years. She had been the chaplain on every main disaster to occur during that time period.

She had served at Ground Zero and the Shanksville PA crash site after 9-11. She had been embedded in Mississippi for months after Hurricane Katrina hit the Gulf Coast. She had trained and equipped more Chaplains and built Corps' over the last 10 years to do the same. Most recently she had deployed to Oklahoma after tornadoes had ripped through.

At home she had delivered death notifications and worked with victims of crime. She trained others and worked diligently to heal her land in the wake of never ending trauma and pain.

She had finally, after so much pain and suffering and light and love and heartache and healing, found her calling. She was a Chaplain. She was called to heal the broken hearted and restore recovery of sight to the blind. She was making Disciples of Christ as a lifestyle and equipping others to do the same.

She was fruitful in her role. She still made mistakes and messes, but the Lord was with her in restoring and redeeming even those things.

She had learned to love because she had found the Love of Christ that worked beyond reason. She had compassion and cared even when it hurt her to do it. She went even when it cost it her something to go. She gave but gained so much more. She was a keeper of the pain and a repairer of the breach as she looked to the Lord to restore and heal others in whatever circumstance. He had never left her nor forsaken her.

CHAPTER 3

THE TRUCK

"Chaplain? It's Ellen from the Sheriff's Office. We have a fatality. Can you head out to the scene?"

"On my way. Do you have any more details?" Meg asked.

"Only that it was a fatality with one male deceased. They said they will brief you when you get there. Not much radio traffic on this one. The Major is out there though with four Deputies. That should tell you something." Ellen said.

Meg knew immediately with the information given that this was going to be a bad one. There are no good fatalities, but there are bad ones, and then there are awful ones. She was afraid this might qualify as the latter.

If the major being on scene wasn't bad enough, the inclusion of three deputies really tipped her off. Under normal circumstances there were only two or three Deputies running on any shift covering an area of 548 square miles.

Meg arrived on scene and radioed in. As she drove, she surveyed the scene. There were several deputies standing in a tight circle to her left and several firemen standing together on the right. It never ceased to amaze her. They were siblings of the same family and for the most part got along where the lines were clear but bumped chests when they overlapped. She was infinitely so proud of both brothers.

She looked again before getting out of her car. Where was the crash? They were standing in a circle, but there was no car and no wreckage. Usually a fatality meant some sort of crash or accident involving a vehicle. She didn't see anything that resembled a crash site. No debris, no vehicle, no smoke. What had happened here?

Meg parked her vehicle behind the ambulance and walked over to the circle of Deputies, assuming her position in the circle.

"Hey guys! I got called for a death notification at a fatality. Where's the crash? What happened?" She asked, head down, mimicking their posture.

"It's not a crash." Deputy Lewis said. "Listen, don't you hear that?"

Meg stood still and listened. Thud. Thud. Thud. Thud. She looked around trying to discern the sound and where it could be coming from. She turned her head towards the source, and her eyes lit on the big Cement truck just off to her right past the firemen. Thud, Thud, Thud, Thud.....

Understanding and horror dawned on her in that moment as she realized that the noise coming from the turning drum on the cement mixer was the sound of a body being churned inside.

"Oh Jesus!" she thought and prayed at the same time. How long had he been going around in there? How long had her deputies been here listening to that? Why hadn't it been turned off? What was the condition of the body now that it was being churned through the blades on the inside of the drum? What do her deputies need right now? Listening to the sound over and over again knowing what was making it made her stomach churn.

"H-h-how long have you guys been here?" she asked, trying not to let her voice betray her horror.

"About 45 minutes. We were told not to touch it and that someone from the company or OSHA or something would be coming.

Yeah, we can't turn it off if that's what you're thinking." The Major said matter-of-factly. His voice was even but his eyes betrayed the stress and nausea they all had to be experiencing.

Another fifteen minutes had passed since she had taken her place in the circle. Her guys were silent for the most part. The press had arrived around the same time she had, so there wasn't much talk or movement on the Deputies' side.

On the Firemen's' side, they had unfolded a tarp and were checking the acetylene torches. Something must be going to happen soon. The tension was palpable. It felt like steam or pressure mounting in a small vessel, and someone was going to have to open the valve and release it into the air.

She had only been here fifteen minutes and she was going crazy at the incessant thud, thud, thud of the body churning in the drum. She could only imagine what her guys were feeling due to the length of time they had been there.

"No one would understand this." She thought, feeling protective. Sometimes the horrific things they faced on a daily basis cried out for a reaction; it's either laugh, scream, cry or run. They used laughter and black humor to endure what they were seeing and to help them cope with what they had to do.

She could feel the veil of tension lifting over the eyes of sorrow, though not completely. Still, it was manageable now. The spring was no longer wound too tight.

She had remembered that particular day after hearing of another one on the news. She remembered the details. How the firemen had cut through the side. She remembered that the cement had poured through the opening; gray tinged with red. She remembered the extrication, the injuries, the cleanup and the transport.

She remembered the death notification she had made to his wife; giving her some details of his injuries. She remembered the look of horror on his wife's face as she learned the circumstances surrounding his death and felt horrified too, but offered comfort and compassion.

She remembered going home and getting sick afterward as she wrote it in her journal. She remembered that it was a long time before she could go back to Taco Bell to eat.

How many years ago was that now? Twelve? It had been a long time.

CHAPTER 4

9-11

Meg stood on the rolling hills just outside Shanksville, PA. She had climbed one of the knolls to get the bigger picture. As she stood there in the breeze she was filled with an overwhelming sense of sadness.

It was so beautiful here. She took in the surrounding hills and trees and tall grass, lush and green, and inhaled deeply. The breeze felt cool on her cheeks. It was fall after all. September 17th, 2001. She turned around and looked in every direction.

"How could anything bad happen here? There is nothing here but nature. How could it happen here?" Meg thought to herself.

She now stood directly facing the Crash site. Flight 93's remains lay spread out in front of her. The trees where the plane had caught fire upon impact hunched scorched and black. She could see the FBI and other workers diligently making their way through the site in their Tyvek suits gridding, mapping, logging and retrieving evidence, personal effects, and body parts.

"Can't fathom it, can you? I mean, how could anything so terrible happen here, right?" said the FBI Chaplain, walking toward her.

"I was just thinking exactly that, my friend, and you're right. I can't fathom this kind of hate. Not that I don't see it every day in some form or fashion but this - I simply don't have words. I just came from Manhattan, worked with the public and spent some time at the pile. It's so unreal." Meg said with a haunted look in her eyes, remembering the last week.

"Well I am glad you're here with your crew. It has been a dark couple of days here too. Lunch is ready if you want to come eat with us. Your crew's already in there."

Meg looked up at him and began to walk alongside him as they made their way down the hill towards the makeshift compound. Meg wasn't sure she could ever describe in words what this past week was like for her or her crew.

September 11th 2001 started out as any other day for Meg. She was up early and heading to the Church where she worked as the Associate Pastor of a small congregation. As usual, she was running late and by now running later after she had stopped to pick up some much needed office supplies.

As she entered the Church with her arms laden down with bags, she was surprised to see a number of people pacing around the Pastor's office. They were watching something on his computer. Meg tried not to disturb them as she headed to her office. It was close to 9:30. Maybe he wouldn't notice that she was late, at least she hoped.

"Meg? Is that you?" Gary, the Senior Pastor, called out.

"Yeah, I just got here. Stopped to pick up the supplies we needed." She said breathlessly.

"Did you see this? I mean, have you been watching this?" he said.

She could tell by the tenor of his voice that something had happened. She made her way to his office where three other parishioners were standing around his desk.

"What are we watching?" she asked.

"Two planes flew into the Twin Towers in New York. We just watched the second one live. It's unbelievable!" Gary said.

"And it's definitely not an accident?" Meg asked. "I mean one could be a malfunction but two….." Meg said staring at the screen showing the plane hit the towers, her voice trailing off, not willing to finish the sentence on everyone's lips; not willing to affirm the unthinkable.

About a minute later, the President stood on TV informing the nation that we were under attack from apparent terrorists. A few more minutes and the news came in that the Pentagon has been hit by flight 77, killing 125 military and civilian personnel.

"I'm going to the SO. I will see you all later." Said Meg as she hurried to retrieve her purse and badge from her office.

Meg made her way to the Sheriff's Office where she found the squad getting briefed on protocols to secure our county and its resources. Possible threat points were identified as well as vulnerable targets. Word came in that a flight came into Ohio airspace, diverted and headed back east.

At 9:59 AM The South Tower of the World Trade Center collapsed with the world watching.

At 10:07 AM Flight 93 crashed into a field in Pennsylvania. It was later learned that it was the flight that had come through Ohio airspace earlier. There were no survivors.

Close to 10:30 AM, Chaplain Meg and the Sheriff and personnel present watched in horror as the North Tower Collapsed. The Sheriff asked Chaplain Meg if she would please lead them in prayer for all involved.

Throughout the rest of the day there were rumors and reports coming in from New York, Pennsylvania, and the Pentagon. The County Law Enforcement agencies were deployed throughout the county to lock down and protect community assets, such as water supplies and power grids. The federal and County Government buildings were secured or evacuated. Chaplain Meg rode along with her deputies as they patrolled with a single minded mission to protect and serve.

Just before 5:30 PM the Seven building at the World Trade Center collapsed after burning for hours.

"Everything has changed now, hasn't it?" Deputy Hanson said. It was a statement; not a question.

"Yes. No going back now. America knows our sense of safety is gone." Meg said. "God is still with us and He is still good. I am glad that we have you guys here. It makes me more grateful for you all. The tale is still being told, but already we are hearing of acts of heroism and selfless acts by cops and firemen protecting and getting people to safety. No one knows how much you guys do and what it costs you to protect us. I'm grateful. I will do whatever I can to help all of you."

Later they learned of the loss of Chaplain Judge from FDNY as one of the towers collapsed on them.

At 8:30 that night President Bush addressed the nation calling the attacks "evil, despicable acts of terror" and declaring that America, its' friends and allies would "stand together to win the war against terrorism."

Meg listened along with her deputies. They all rallied, and a sense of resolve settled over them. A renewed sense of patriotism and community had begun to be built. We may have been hit, but our flag still flew and we were still here and we had a President who was a leader and just as resolved in this moment to lead us out of woundedness and into strength to fight and protect our homeland. We were sucker punched and determined to not let that happen again.

"Meg, it's May. I'm picking you up, ok? You at the SO?" The LT asked.

"Yeah. You coming in or you want me to meet you on the pad?" Meg asked.

"I'm coming in. See you in two."

Meg waited in the break room with a couple other deputies. May came in like always with her banter about SO versus PD. Meg always sided with her deputies. She bled black and gold and blue, she teased. It was all good natured though, and they gave as good as they got. May was a well-respected member of the LEO family. She had earned a reputation for integrity and hard work. She never hesitated to give God the glory for her success. Everyone knew she was a believer and respected that she walked the walk. She was also a very tough cookie with high standards in work ethic and conduct for her officers, which sometimes made relationships tough.

May dropped off some paperwork and asked the guys how they were holding up. They talked for a few minutes and then she asked Meg if she was ready to roll. They ended up a local restaurant that they frequented. They didn't even have to order; the waitresses just brought them their drinks and asked what kind of night it was - food or pie - and brought their food accordingly. Tonight was definitely a "both" kind of night!

` "I want us to go to New York." May said. "I think we need to be there."

"Ok. I will pray about it too. Right now God has us here to help calm. If He is calling us to go then He will make a way. We are going to need some money for sure but it would be nice to take some needed stuff too." Meg said. "Let's pray and see what He has for us."

Late in the night Meg was still up processing all that had happened that day. She had her Bible open, but wasn't able to concentrate. She was watching the events unfold on TV and listening to the stories of those who were there. The terror and confusion overwhelming people.

"Ask May if she still wants to go to New York." She knew the voice of the Lord immediately in her head.

"Lord are you sure?" Meg asked shyly.

"Ask May if she still wants to go to New York."

"Yes Lord." Meg said. She was confident that the Lord was making a way for His purposes to be fulfilled and with that she knew He would provide for it.

Meg didn't wait, she called May right away and told her what the Lord had spoken. Her reply was immediate.

"Yeah I wanna go! What do we need to do?" She asked.

"I don't know where He is taking us yet but we will need money and supplies and transportation. He has it already for us we just need to put it out there. Just like when Jesus told His disciple go and tell the man with donkey colt that the Master has need of it we need to do the same. The Master has need of them."

Within three days they had over $5000 in cash, three van loads of supplies and thirteen people, a secure place to stay and were heading to Manhattan.

Over the next several days, the tiny troop worked and lived with a Church on East 9th street. They worked with the old and newly homeless, and tirelessly ministered to all who had need. In the evenings they would make their way to Union Square and join in the spontaneous worship and throngs of people praying or needing just to be together. Meg and May were able to work the pile as well with other Law Enforcement and Military personnel. God was there and was still good. That was the message of hope they conveyed everywhere they set their feet.

CHAPTER 5

MEG

Meg sat at her table eating breakfast and trying to finish her homework. She was behind again and needed desperately to catch up. The end of the semester was fast approaching. Time Management was her constant nemesis! She was a wife and mother working as the Associate Pastor at the church, going to seminary and now had added Sheriff's Chaplain to her already full plate. She had spent another night out in the Cruisers with her Deputies as they patrolled the County. She was busier than she'd ever been in her life, and she loved every breathless moment of it.

People had been telling her for years that they were worried that she was going to burn out and her reply had always been the same…she said she would rather wear out than rust out… she had always relished in carrying a heavy burden. She was passionate about God and His purposes and about His passion for people. Most people misunderstood her passion for ambition and viewed it as a negative thing.

She struggled long and hard with that misunderstanding, but settled the fact with God even if people were contentious with her. She knew who she was in Christ and was good with it, and that sent most people for a loop anyway. She had spent a long time being miserable trying to conform to other people's ideas and expectations of what she should be. Thankfully God has a higher thought and a higher purpose that men will never see unless they seek Him in it. Meg was a seeker of a higher thought of God every day and for the most part she found it.

"Mom?"

Meg looked up from her book and looked over at her beautiful redheaded Sara, her Sara. She was a beauty! Every time Meg saw her in the light she marveled that God would give her such a creature! Sara possessed a sensitive soul as well. She was concerned for others in a profoundly honest way. She was an "old soul" in that even at a young age she intuitively sensed the depth of people's souls; their wants and needs and desires and potentials. That, Meg knew, was a gift from God even when it sometimes felt like a curse to her Sara.

"Yeah Baby? What's up?" Meg asked smiling.

"There is this girl, Jade, that works with me and she is, like, 8 months pregnant. She and her boyfriend, Jeff live in this little apartment on the avenues and they have nothing - I mean nothing - yet for the baby. They are really poor and they both work but there is just not enough for anything extra. Do you think we could do something?" Sara asked hopefully.

"Sure. Let me talk to the Senior Pastor and see if we can put together a baby shower at the church. I think this is a great opportunity for some outreach, you know, show some real love. Let me go see what I can get put together."

Meg was on a mission now. She was excited at the prospect of helping someone in need and to welcome a new life as well. God had given her a perspective a long time ago not to let people's circumstances circumvent the purposes of God to draw people to Him. After all, she had been a throw away and He went to extraordinary measures to woo her into His kingdom.

Meg headed over to the church and dropped her bag off in her office and headed to the Senior Pastor's office. She found him wrestling with cords and electrical cables, trying to hook up the newly arrived computer.

"Can I give you a hand?" she asked, smiling. They both knew she was of absolutely no use in this situation as she was a technodolt. The most she could do was hold something and stare at him blankly when he asked for it.

"No, I got it sorted out now." He replied.

"Pastor, I have a request when you have a minute. There's this great opportunity for outreach and possibly evangelism. I would like to run it past you." Meg knew that using the words "outreach and evangelism" would peak his interest.

"Give me a half hour and then we can sit down and talk about it."

Meg went back to her office and started on her tasks for the day. She was in various states of doneness on a variety of projects and correspondence as well as her homework. Two hours later the Pastor called her over to his office. He had laboriously finished putting the computer together. She knew that now that there was a semblance of order she would have his attention fully.

Meg launched into conveying Sara's request. She told him that she felt that it was a perfect opportunity to show the love of Christ to this couple and to welcome this new life about to be born. What a great thing it would be to shower them with the very things that were needed and necessary while truly showing them that they and their child are valued and seen by being God's hands extended.

The Pastor stood up and started shuffling papers on his desk, his brows furrowed.

"No, absolutely not. If you do it for one you will have to do it for all." He said sternly.

"I don't understand. What would be wrong with that?" Meg asked confused.

"We aren't going to condone sin, and if we do it here for an out of wedlock situation then we will be giving the appearance that we approve and for the record...we do not." He eyed her with - was that contempt she saw?

Meg felt her ire rising. "I'm sorry. I thought we were supposed to be leading people out of sin by introducing them to Jesus. How do we do that if we aren't allowing them in? You won't have a problem if I do it at my house then right?"

"I can't control what you do in your house but I am cautioning you." He said looking away.

"That's exactly right. You can't control what I do in my home." She said emphasizing the word "control".

"I have a lunch appointment. Is there anything else you need right now?" He said with his back angled towards her.

"Nope. I'm good. I will be working here finishing up some paperwork. Have a good lunch." Meg could feel the tension radiating from him. *This is not good.* She thought.

Over the next two days Meg, May and Sara worked hard to get a baby shower pulled together for that weekend. Time was short after all. There were only a few short weeks before the baby would be here and they wanted to make sure that it arrived with everything it needed to give it the best possible start. They wanted to relieve as much stress from the young parents-to-be as possible.

The day of the baby shower arrived with a phenomenal turnout. May had gotten a lot of ladies from her church to come and they showed up in spades. A few from Meg's church bravely showed as well. The Pastor had not spoken directly about not attending but had made it very clear that he did not approve. His wife was in attendance, most likely to keep an eye on who had showed up. Meg was hopeful that she would be able to smooth it over later when they realized that helping someone in need could never be a disservice to the church.

Meg was overjoyed by the turnout! The baby would want for nothing when it arrived. The ladies had gone all out. There was a crib, the layette, the sheets, a pack-n-play, diapers, bottles, onesies, sleepers, stroller, car seat, toys, and shampoos, creams, lotions and wipes. There was nothing missing as far as necessities.

This is God's way. Meg thought. *He overflows His goodness through His people and overwhelms with His love. There is no defense against the onslaught of grace shown through the love of His people trying to woo one into the kingdom. They are giving abundantly because they know the abundance of the love you have shown them when they were in the middle of their circumstances. Thank you for this opportunity, Lord and may there be fruit that remains from this day.*

After all the gifts had been opened and the party games played, it came time to send Jade and Jeff on their way. Jade could not contain her tears of gratitude and appreciation as Meg, Sara and May loaded everything up into the van. Jeff was smiling but reserved. Jade continued crying through the procession of hugs and thank you's.

"Hey," Meg said, "We would love to stay involved. Please call us if you need anything and we will be happy to help. You have some seasoned moms here too who have all kinds of tips and tricks! Seriously though, will you call when you go into labor so we can at least be praying and hopefully be able to see the little guy when he gets here?"

Jade nodded and beamed a smile that could light up a city.

"If you would like to attend a church sometime I'm sure one of the ladies from May's church would be happy to take you, I mean, if you would like to go." Meg stammered. She was embarrassed because she knew after her conversation with the senior pastor that she couldn't take her to hers.

"I don't believe in that God stuff but Jade can go if she wants to." Jeff said matter-of-factly.

"It's all good!" Meg said, giving Jeff and Jade a quick squeeze. "We are here for you in whatever capacity you want. We just want

to be there for you and the little guy. Diapers-r-us if nothing else!"
she said laughing.

With that Jade and Jeff got in the van and pulled out of the
driveway with a wave heading home to prepare for their precious
gift about to arrive.

CHAPTER 6
JADE

"Mom I can't go!" her Sara wailed.

"Can't go where? Baby what's wrong? Are you hurt?" Meg asked with rising concern.

"I can't go! Can you go, Mom? Please!" Sara asked with increasing panic.

"What's wrong, Baby? Tell me what's happening! Go where?" The woman pleaded. This whole conversation was out of character for her Sara. Her strong, smart, confident Sara didn't panic and the sound in her voice was just that; panic.

"Jade's in the hospital having the baby and they are telling her that the baby is dead. Mom, I can't go! Can you go?" The pain and panic in her Sara's voice as she said out loud what was so painful to even consider was heartbreaking.

"I'll go, baby. I'm on my way." Meg hung up the phone and headed back over to her table.

"Sorry to cut and run but I have a thing I gotta do." She said as she grabbed her coat from the back of the chair.

Meg had been enjoying her time with her officers around the table as they ate and joked and decompressed from the successful drug raid that they had just completed. She had been their Chaplain for a few months now and was just learning the nuances and dynamics. It was a very different experience with this group.

Meg had come to this small town almost a year ago to take a position as an Associate Pastor at a church there. She was finishing up her third year of Bible Institute at the same time. A twist of circumstance brought her here to this table now. She had served as a Volunteer Chaplain in a State Prison for 6 years prior to becoming a Pastor, but had never considered Chaplaincy as a main ministry let alone being the Sheriff's Chaplain.

"May can I talk to you?" She asked the LT sitting next to her. The LT got up and walked with her to the cashier stand.

"What's up?" May asked.

"Do you remember the woman, Jade, that we had the baby shower for about a month ago?" Meg asked.

"Yeah. Is she having the baby?" May asked, getting excited.

"My Sara just called me and told me that Jade is at the hospital having the baby but they are telling her that the baby is dead." Meg paused and stared hard at May, letting it sink in. "I'm heading over there now."

"Let me get my coat." May said moving quickly back to the table. Meg paid the check and was waiting by the door.

"I'll start calling some people and get them praying. What else do you know?" May said.

"Nothing yet. That was all Sara seemed to know. I don't even know who called her. She is really taking this hard. She is still at work too so that makes it worse. At least she can keep busy while she's waiting for news. Let's roll and I guess we'll see when we get there."

Meg and May left the restaurant and walked out into the night. It was after midnight and it was cold and dark. No moon tonight. No clouds either. Meg looked up for a moment and saw the stars in the clear black sky and silently asked God to guide her and help her because she didn't know what to do. "This is too big for me, Lord!" Came the cry from her very soul. "But it's not too big for you." With that she got into her car and headed to the hospital, not knowing where this was going to lead.

CHAPTER 7

BABY GREGORY

Meg had been thinking back on that day just three short weeks ago as she drove silently to the hospital. It had been a day so full of joy, promise and hope. How could it be so sad and hopeless now? As Meg drove, May spoke on the phone giving information and instructions to her prayer group. The Woman wondered if she should call anyone from her church but felt she should let May do her thing. For the life of her she couldn't think of anyone to call. Her mind was running through her recent chaplain training and her almost three years of seminary school, trying to grasp ahold of what she should do or say when she got to the hospital, but she was drawing a blank. She had nothing. She began to pray silently and asked God to show her what she needed to do. She questioned whether she was the right person to help in this situation. Was He truly asking her to be His representative for grieving parents? Surely there had to be someone more qualified, more prepared, more anything than her. After all, in her heart of hearts she was crying out for understanding herself so how could she be expected to bring understanding to others?

Meg and May made their way into the hospital and rushed to the Maternity Ward. May was still on the phone so Meg went to the desk and spoke with the nurse.

"Hi. I'm Chaplain Meg and I am here for Jade. Can you tell me what room she is in?" Meg inquired breathlessly.

"I'm glad you're here." The nurse said handing Meg a box. "Here you go. She's in room 312."

Meg stared at the box and then looked back at the nurse. "Umm…what's all this?" Meg asked feeling stupid.

"She registered as Catholic so that's what you will need."

"There's no priest coming, or a nun?" Meg asked.

"No. They aren't married and they are not members of the local diocese. I'm heading back in there and I will let them know you are here." With that the nurse headed back down the hall.

Meg felt the frustration mounting inside her just as it had the day she had spoken to the Senior Pastor about the baby shower. She realized that there was something rotten running down through the core of denominational religion. Jesus would not have turned Jade away. There were more than enough examples in the red letters of the book to turn to.

Meg picked up the box and took it to the waiting room where May was sitting. Meg sat the box in a chair and took off her coat. She stared at the box for some time trying to comprehend what had just happened here. Finally she reached in and began to explore the contents. Inside there were laminated cards with prayers and rituals and ceremonies. There was a flask of holy water and a bottle of anointing oil. There were some things that Meg did not recognize as well. She called May over and asked her if she recognized the items, hoping she get some insight because May had been raised Catholic.

After sorting through the box and putting some things together, Meg felt a little better, but still didn't have a clue as to what order these things were to be performed in or whether they would even accept them from her because she was neither Catholic nor a Priest. Meg knew that prepared or not, at some point she must walk through that door and do something.

Meg looked over at May. "I have some people coming and I'm going to meet them in the lobby and we will be praying. Do you need anything?" May asked.

I need someone who is more prepared for this than I am, Meg thought.

"No. You go. I'm going in in a minute." Meg said, trying to hide the strain and wariness in her voice.

"I'll bring you up some water in a little bit. Call when you need it or if you need anything." May said as she walked to elevator.

Meg didn't reply. She sat there for a minute. She was alone and felt every bit of it. Her thoughts were continually looping between "God I don't understand why this is happening!" and "This is too big for me! Did you send the right one? Are you sure?" At some point in the midst of all the chaos in her mind a single quiet sentence formed.

"And David encouraged himself in the Lord."

Meg's breath caught in her throat. She grabbed onto the words and knew what she had to do. She stilled herself and forced her mind to quiet. Silently she communed with God. "Lord, I am willing and am nothing besides obedient. I will do whatever you ask me to do. I am also afraid. This is too big for me but it is not too big for you. Whatever you need me to do I will do. Do not let me fail or faint no matter the news. As long as you are with me I will walk. I know there must be a purpose but I don't understand any of this right now but I will trust you and I will walk. You have to help me, I am afraid but I will walk."

Meg stood and picked up the box and held it in front of her. Therein lay her purpose for walking into that room. She held the box like a shield in front of her tight against her chest and taking a deep breath, she walked in the room.

She faded from the dim light of the hallway into the bright, manufactured, piercing light of Jade's room. She squinted a little as her eyes adjusted. Jade's family filled the room. They were talking and laughing and Meg could tell that they were still holding out hope.

Meg surveyed the room as she walked slowly toward the place where Jeff was standing. She noticed several things right away as she said hello to those she passed. First she noticed the bassinet. It was sterile looking. There were no brightly colored blankets or goodie bags or even diapers in preparation to receive a newborn. It was empty and cold. It sat there almost as an indictment of the truth. Meg quickly hurried past it. Next she noticed that there was no sound. No fetal heartbeat monitor, no heartbeat. Meg felt the prickle of goosebumps rising on her arms, and she silently communed with God..."don't let me faint, Lord, let me finish what you sent me here for." Immediately she felt the warmth of His presence and was comforted. Thanking the Holy Spirit for His immediacy, she continued to walk.

Meg made her way around the group until she was standing next to Jeff. She marveled at how big he was. She hadn't noticed before. They were standing next to Jade's bed, where Jade was sleeping by the window. Meg sat the box down on the windowsill behind her and rubbed Jeff's shoulder, thinking about how when she had been the most lost, God had sent her a stack of boxes to help ease her pain. The irony and the journey were not lost on her; He had once given her her own boxes to open, and through his light and love she could now help others in need with their own boxes.

"How you holding up, big guy?" Meg asked, trying not to sound overly familiar.

"I'm doing ok. I'm just worried about her." Jeff choked out, watching Jade.

Jade's eyes fluttered open with a start. Meg and Jeff rushed towards the bed in a single movement. As Jade opened her eyes she rolled her head toward Jeff and Meg, and when her eyes met

Meg's she did the most unexpected thing; she smiled - not just a hello smile, but that big beaming light a city up smile; Meg's heart skipped a beat and she took two steps backward before gaining her composure.

Meg's mind was reeling. On the inside she was melting down. How could this be! It shouldn't be happiness to see me here now under these circumstances! God you have to help me! I don't understand! On the outside she was moving closer with a smile of her own.

Meg leaned down and kissed Jade on the cheek. "How you doing, Baby?" She asked, surprised that her voice sounded so steady.

"I'm ok. I'm not feeling much they gave me an epidural." Jade said.

"Well that's good. Can I get you anything? Ice chips…want me get you a fresh wash cloth for your face? Anything?" Meg trailed off feeling helpless and inadequate. Jade just shook her head and said that she was fine.

After a few uncomfortable minutes of silence and staring Meg asked, "Would you like me to pray?"

Jade smiled and said, "Yes, please."

Meg gathered herself together inside. She had never prayed those prayers that she heard so often from those around her. She was as Pentecostal as they come, but she never prayed a prayer where she demanded God comply or pushed Him around. She knew Him as sovereign and Holy and could never approach Him as if He were common or a like a buddy. Even now she approached Him like the Divine Majestic Most Holy God. She didn't ask Him to fix it, she didn't ask Him to change it, she asked Him for what they all needed right this moment.

She asked Him to come. She asked Him to fill this place with His tangible presence and peace. She asked Him who knows the end from the beginning to bring comfort and understanding and to show Himself mighty so that others might believe and know the goodness of His grace. She asked for Him to come…and He did. Everyone in the room felt it at the same time. His presence filled the room with a tangible, bright, all-consuming warmth. Everyone responded to it differently. For some tears flowed silently down their cheeks. For others they wondered out loud about what was happening. Still yet others left the room unable to stand up under it.

Meg finished her prayer. Even with the tangible presence of God surrounding her, she kissed Jade on the cheek and fled the room like a coward. As she reached the waiting room she sat on the chair and communed with God and said yet again, *I don't understand, you have to help me! I'm so sorry if I am the weakest link and I am afraid. I know you are here but I don't know what to do!*

Meg sat there for a while feeling frustrated, inadequate and useless. The Holy Spirit began to break through as He brought to her remembrance other times when she had been afraid and God had shown up on her behalf. She remembered that in each of those situations the outcome had not been what she expected or wanted, but that it had proven to be a better outcome even with the pain than she could ever have foreseen herself. She was trusting Him that this would be no different. She called May and gave her an update. Then for the next 3 hours she sat outside the room listening to a woman in labor giving birth to a baby she knew was dead. The process had to continue. A birth was coming.

The nurse walked out of the room. Meg jumped up, eyes seeking answers from the nurse's face. The tears were the most telling. Neither she nor the nurse spoke a word but Meg knew. She and the nurse hugged each other in the hallway for a minute. As they broke apart they both knew they still had work to do.

Meg went back to the chair and retrieved her box. She called May and told her what had not been spoken but known. After she hung up she sighed. "Lord, I will walk." She said. She could hear the sadness and the resolve in her voice. She felt very tired all of the sudden. The woman straightened her back, took a deep breath and picked up her box. She positioned again tight against her body like a shield and walked through the door one more time.

Meg once again surveyed the room. This time Jade's family members were crying quietly. Tears flowed and the grief was heavy in the room. Meg looked first to the bassinet. It was empty. She walked steadily past the grieving family. She touched them as she walked and said, "I'm so sorry." She was thankful that they didn't ask her anything because she didn't have any answers. What was one supposed to say? She would rather be silent than give a bumper sticker theology answer that is oh so useless and utterly unhelpful in times of such deep grief and loss.

Meg had made her way to where Jeff was standing beside Jade next to the window. Meg sat the box on the windowsill again just like before. The whole situation felt surreal. Was this really happening? Was she really here? She shook the thoughts away and concentrated. She needed to see and to hear right now.

Jeff stood very still with his arms crossed around himself. He looked like he was trying to literally hold himself together. Meg could see that he was trying to be strong, but that it wouldn't be long before he lost it. Meg reached out and touched his shoulder but couldn't speak. It was here that she learned "if you can't improve on silence, don't try." She could feel the tension in his body.

Meg looked over at the bed where Jade was sitting up. She moved closer. Jade looked up at her with tears streaming unhindered down her face.......and she smiled......

Meg grabbed and held tight to the bedrail. "What is that? Why is she smiling at me like that? Oh, God, I don't understand! Help me!" On the outside, Meg leaned in and kissed Jade on the cheek. In Jade's arms she held the most beautiful, perfect baby boy; and he was dead. Meg was awed by the sight of him. "Oh Jade! He's beautiful!" she exclaimed.

Again her mind reeled. He was perfect, he was beautiful.... how could he be dead? She knew it was true. The proof was in front of her, she was staring at it in the face of that cold, beautiful baby boy.

Jade cuddled him, staring intensely at his face. She was memorizing every line and every feature. She knew she didn't have long. She patted him and cooed softly, as the tears continued to flow down her cheeks. Jeff stood beside her bed moving restlessly from foot to foot. He was staring too; from his son's face to that of his beloved Jade. Grief, concern, confusion and pain jockeyed for the prime position in his eyes and heart. He was shaking now. Meg reached behind her to the box and fished out a laminated card.

She stood up and said to everyone, "If it's ok with all of you I would like to get started." She waited as they gathered and came around the bed. Jeff seemed to grow calmer at this point. Meg looked at the card, noting that it read "Naming Ceremony".

Meg gathered her wits and thanked God silently for the one who put this box together with everything outlined. She began to read from the card and followed it step by step. She spoke the prayer and read the scriptures provided. At one point she was instructed to take the infant from his mother and place him in his father's arms for naming.

Meg picked up the child. She cradled him in her arms. She could feel his weight, the substance. She stared at him too, memorizing every line, every feature. She thought to herself, "Is anyone ever going to know you were here? Will no one outside this room ever remember you?" She made a vow right then and there that she would. She finished anointing his head with oil and handed him to his father. Jeff held him as if he were the most precious thing in the world; and he was. Jeff's large, rough hands encompassed his son in a protective embrace and he held him close to his chest and kissed his cheek.

"What do you name your son?" Meg asked, her voice cracking with the emotion of the moment.

"Gregory Aaron." Jeff replied. His voice was strong and clear.

"So shall he be named on earth and in heaven received of the Father, Gregory Aaron." Meg said just as strong and just as clear. She finished the prayer and scripture readings from the card. She took baby Gregory back in her arms and sprinkled him with water and gave him back to his mother.

And like a coward… she fled the room.

There were more cards and more rituals and more, more, more but she couldn't do it. She ran into the hallway and grief overcame her. She stared at the ceiling and in her soul cried out, "Father you have to help me! This is too big for me! I don't understand! Help me understand!"

From behind her she heard Jeff yell her name. "Meg!"

"Oh no, he knows I didn't do it right and he's going to kill me now!" She thought wildly. Meg turned to see Jeff bounding toward her reaching out. She was momentarily terrified, but he wrapped her in a warm bear hug. Jeff was sobbing and shaking as he held on to her. She was having trouble holding them both up. Meg was holding on to him just as hard as he was holding her. Suddenly he pulled back and had her by her shoulders and he was shaking her intensely.

"Tell me! Tell me!!" He shouted.

"Tell you what, Jeff?" Meg asked. "Tell you what?" Inside she had nothing to say. What was she supposed to say? She didn't understand herself!

"Tell me how I can get ahold of God so I can see my son again!" Jeff said sobbing and pulling her close again. "Tell me what I have to do."

Meg straightened up. "Oh Lord, now I understand. This child did more in his brief moments on this earth than most of us do from the pew in a lifetime. He led his father to the knowledge of God. This I can do, I can show him the way to see his son again."

Meg and Jeff went down on their knees in the hallway and she explained salvation and led Jeff through the prayer. A few days later after the funeral, Meg was privileged to lead Jade to the Lord as well. She married them in the light of God, and has now celebrated the births of their healthy, happy children. Baby Gregory is still remembered and is spoken of often as a testimony to the power of God to save, redeem and heal.

PART 2
MOUNTAINS TO CLIMB

CHAPTER 8
BEGINNINGS

It was finally sunny! It had rained for two days straight and she'd been cooped up in the house. Now here she sat in her yard, warmed by the soft April sunshine, nestled between her Barbie doll and her watering can. Standing, she walked very carefully across the yard carrying her treasure. She only spilled a little bit of the water when she startled a bee lazily stirring in the grass.

The grass and clover glistened, pushing away from the damp ground. Her favorite place was the apple tree down by the creek. There were five Apple trees in the yard, but this one was hers. She rooted around inside the hollow of the tree to find the pennies she had planted there. She found herself wishing very much that it would turn into a money tree, like her Pap had said.

As for Meg, she was a little thing. She had short brown hair and big brown eyes. The only girl in her family, she had two big brothers and new baby brother who had been born just that winter. She retreated her to her tree when she could. It was quiet there. In the house it was never quiet unless her father was home; it was understood that when his tall shadow covered the floor of the house, the children were to be still and quiet. Her mother made sure that was understood and enforced.

The Mother had a way of making herself understood. Even at her age, Meg knew when to disappear. The Mother yelled, and the mother hit, in a never-ending pattern that was as terrifying as it was predictable.

Meg was frightened of The Mother. The two days in the house with the rain were filled with yelling and hitting. The Mother worked in the family store adjacent to the house with her father, but would come back inside the house regularly. Most of the time, the children were relegated to the yard when the weather was good.

But today, Meg was happy to be outside. All of the rainy anxiety beating around her chest was finally free to escape into the earth and the trees and the sky outside.

Meg sat, diligently thumbing through her planted pennies. Suddenly, she snapped out of her distracted reverie to the sound of panting right behind her. She jumped when she felt the cold wet nose and a lick on the back of her arm. She turned around to see her neighbor's beagle puppy hopping and dancing around her. She giggled and squealed as the puppy jumped on her. She rolled on the ground as it continued its' wet, ticklish assault on her face.

The neighbor boy wasn't far behind the dog, holding a collar and leash. He moved in abrupt, awkward, jerking motions. Meg knew there was something wrong with him and that he had to see the doctor a lot but she didn't know what it was about. Everyone knew. She heard the women talking with The Mother about it a lot when they were in the store. They always seemed sad about it.

"Hey! You caught him for me!" He said, panting as he finally reached her. As she looked up at him, the sun caught her eyes, making her squint. He was tall to her, though he was only about 12 or 13. Meg giggled as the puppy continued to jump and dance. Sam began to laugh too as Meg and puppy rolled around on the ground.

"Want to help me get him home?" He asked smiling down at her. "I'm taking him on a walk first, if you want to come."

Meg jumped up and helped Sam fasten the collar and leash onto the rowdy puppy, and they headed out of the yard and onto the shaded, residential street. Meg chatted incessantly as they walked beneath the warm dappled light of the trees. She told Sam about the pennies and what she had made she told him that she was going to go to kindergarten soon, and she told him about the noisy baby brother who cried at night. He was easy to talk to.

Sam led and Meg followed, holding onto the leash as the puppy pulled her along. At some point Meg became alarmed, realizing that she didn't know where she was. She began to get scared, and asked Sam to take her back home. Her mother and brothers would be waiting, and the sun was starting to dip down below the tractor trailers around them.

Sam wouldn't answer her, but instead grabbed her by the arm and pushed her down to the ground under the trailer. She lost her grip on the leash and the puppy ran off, yelping in alarm.

Now Meg was frightened, crying and asking for her mother. Her whole body hurt from being yanked down and slammed into the earth she had just been so happy to warm herself on. She begged Sam to take her back home. Instead he pushed her roughly onto her stomach and pressed her face onto the ground. She began to scream and flail as dirt and dust filled her mouth, but he told her not to or she wouldn't see her mother again. Meg stopped screaming, but couldn't still the tears rolling from her cheeks and pooling in small muddy puddles under her face. She felt Sam tug at her clothes roughly and clumsily. She felt the cool air hit her skin as her pants came down around her ankles. He had one hand on the back of her neck pushing her face into the dirt as he tugged at her panties with the other one. Meg felt a paralyzing fear grip every muscle in her body. She tried to kick, but something heavy was on her legs. She cried and cried as she felt his hand move over her buttocks and waist. They suddenly seemed so course and rough. She didn't understand why he was hurting her.

At some point, through the haze, she realized that she could hear her mother calling her name. She zeroed in on the sound, like a lighthouse beam cutting through fog. The Mother was coming for her. She became numb to the pain and the weight on her body, and focused on The Mother's voice. The horrible sensation crawled inside her and seemed to last forever. She felt something hard rubbing against the backs of her thighs, and then suddenly something hot, wet and sticky. She wondered if the puppy had come back but couldn't move to see.

Suddenly, Meg saw something move out of the corner of her eye. Her oldest brother's head popped out from under the trailer, and she saw his eyes grow as huge as dinner saucers. Relief washed over her like a warm wave. He would take her home!

The Brother jumped up and ran away, leaving Meg in the dust. The last bit of hope swam away from her, as Sam jumped up and ran away too, leaving her on the ground, alone in a puddle of the dirt, his sweat, and her tears.

Meg tried to get up but she was so tired from crying and struggling. She couldn't see because of the thick film of tears and dust clouding her eyelashes. As she struggled to get off her stomach, the pain was more than she could take and as she tried to stand, she kept falling around her pants, bunched up at her ankles. She managed to flip over to a sitting position, and tugged at her clothes, trying to get them on. She felt the sticky wet stuff on her legs as she sat in the dirt and tried to wipe it off in the grass.

She was finally able to stand, on legs as wobbly as a newborn foal, and as she started to walk and tug her pants on, she felt so tired and shaky that she toppled over several times. She thought only of home through the haze of her hurt and her tears. She ran; not knowing where she was going, she still ran, in the direction she had heard The Mother's voice.

She made it to her yard and ran for the house, now never wanting to leave its' warm inside. A sense of relief washed over her with unexpected force as she finally made it into the house. The tears were coming uncontrollably now, dam broken, as she saw The Mother pacing with a phone in her hand. The Mother hung up quickly. Meg reached for The Mother seeking comfort, consolation and relief. Instead The Mother shook her, and yelled at her. She dragged her to her room and whipped her with a belt and roughly shoved Meg into her bed. The Mother left, slamming the door behind.

Hurt, dazed, and confused, Meg laid on her pillow and cried and cried thinking that she had been bad and that she had done something wrong. Finally she cried herself to sleep whispering softly to herself, "I'm sorry mommy!"

A while later, The Mother came into the room, and yanked her from her bed, shoving her roughly to the bathroom. The tub was already filled and The Mother stripped Meg quickly and placed her in the steaming, scalding water. Meg cried as the water hit her wounds. The Mother said nothing as she scrubbed Meg with a washcloth. Meg could feel The Mother's anger and tried not to cry out with each hurtful scrub. She was ashamed and confused. The Mother roughly jerked her out of the tub and rubber her raw skin unceremoniously with a towel. Meg stepped into clean clothes and The Mother gathered the towel, the washcloth and her dirty ones. She let the water out of the tub and walked from the room without a word.

Meg knew she was in trouble as she left the bathroom. The raw anger was plain on The Mother's face. Meg knew better than to say anything. She walked in a haze into the kitchen, and The Mother gave her a sandwich and told her to sit down and eat.

Every word was cold and curt. Meg did as she was told and devoured the sandwich. She was so hungry! She slurped down the glass of milk and wanted more but didn't dare ask for it. When she was done, The Mother took her plate and cup and slammed them into the sink, washing them in silence. Meg sat very still, not knowing what to do. Finally The Mother turned to her and told her to go play outside but not to leave the yard again or she would get another whipping. And then The Mother said, "Don't tell your father about what happened today."

Meg went back outside to her tree and sat down next to her Barbie and her watering can right where she left them and hugged herself and cried.

Over the next 10 years Meg endured constant and consistent abuse from The Mother. The Mother's hitting was frequent but the verbal assaults were the most damaging. Meg was told she was stupid, and berated by The Mother and both Older Brothers continually.

Meg, now fourteen, was always angry. The sweet little girl with her watering can had stayed in the hollow of the apple tree, with the pennies, and a harder, sadder, damaged Meg had come out. She was always either in a fight or starting one. She was skipping school and had become aggressive. Her anger was the only emotion that she knew and felt. She was numb to anything else. At one point, while talking loudly and crudely. Her cousin had told her that she was disrespectful and a menace. Meg laughed at her and said something awful. The cousin never talked to her again.

Meg was miserable inside, but she learned to live and act in survival mode. There were few people she was close or kind to. The ones that tolerated her or were indifferent to her, and vice versa, were like her; separated, abused, alone. Meg lived in a world where the best emotion towards her was tolerance. None of those people were connected to anyone else or attached to anything else. Nothing mattered. They just existed, floated on the tide of the tedium. They were like shadows, vapor that dissipated when you looked directly at it.

She learned early on that there was a sightline, and that she was below it. How many times has she come to school bruised and battered but no one cared, no one asked, no one looked. When she had a black eye from The Brother she intentionally looked at a teacher directly in the face to make him see her. She couldn't say she was surprised when he looked at her and then quickly looked somewhere else and walked away. Invisible, alone and angry, she felt herself hoping that this was how it was for everyone, although she knew that wasn't true. She just knew that *she* had no value to anyone. She remembered witnessing one of the normal girls who had skinned her knee on the concrete get all kinds of attention from teachers and kids. And she wasn't even bleeding! Meg knew that there was a difference between her and the normal girl. The normal girl mattered; Meg was below the sight line and this girl was above it.

Her anger and tension grew daily as The Brother became more and more aggressive and violent with her. Now he was doing whatever he could to humiliate her at school, too. There was no relief, no haven, no help, and no hope.

The most recent violent episode had involved him smashing her face into the bed frame. She fought back as she always did, but she was never as strong as The Brother. She'd gotten "uppity" with him and that was not allowed. She hit and scratched at him until he retreated because of the noise she was making. The next day he struck as she was setting her book bag in her room after school. He came from behind and put her in a choke hold and bashed her head into the headboard. She knew eventually he was going to kill her, but she wasn't going to die today! The Mother was due home soon and Meg knew that he would not do anything more than hit her or push her when she was around.

Meg had been dazed, and the pain from her head hitting the headboard caused her instant nausea. She was dizzy and couldn't breathe from the hold he had on her throat. She clawed his arm and tried to kick his legs but he was too well practiced and seemed quite impervious to any pain she may have caused. At that point the younger brother came in and though he tried to help Meg, he wasn't strong enough. The Brother let go of Meg and laughed at her and the younger brother. He punched the younger brother hard and left the room.

Meg had gasped for air and yelled at the younger brother to leave her alone. She was so ashamed at her weakness and what he saw. She still remembered a look of confusion and anger on his face as he yelled back at her and left. Meg sat on her bed seething. The Mother was home now she could hear the younger brother telling her all that had happened. Now The Mother was yelling for Meg to "get down here!" Angry, Meg stomped down the stairs. She wasn't frightened of The Mother anymore; she didn't feel anything except anger. The Mother demanded an explanation. Meg told her that The Brother came into the room, choked her and bashed her head into the headboard. The Mother asked Meg what she had done. Angry Meg screamed at The Mother, "nothing, as usual!"

At this point The Brother sauntered down the stairs heading for the kitchen. Meg could feel the goose egg forming on her head and her anger grew as he smugly smirked at her and pushed past her. The wave within her finally broke on the shore. She began to yell at The Mother, "Why won't you help me! You know what he does to me! Why won't you do something?!" The Mother just looked at Meg and said flatly, "if you can't defend yourself I can't help you." and then just walked away. Meg wasn't done yet. She flew into the kitchen where The Mother and The Brother were and she screamed at The Brother," why do you do it? Why do you hate me so much! Why don't you just both get it over with and finish it just kill me then!" The Brother just laughed and told Meg that she wasn't worth the bullet. The Mother paused for just a moment and in silence began getting dinner ready. Meg realized that there was truly no hope for her and inside herself, she let go and went completely dead. She didn't even feel the anger anymore.

Meg went through the motions of life in the shadow land. She went to school, played in the band, but was consistently humiliated by The Brother. Now she would do things to make him embarrassed or to make him mad, even knowing that the price was more beatings. She did it because she had a little control knowing he would have to restrain himself in public. She became more aggressive with him and that infuriated him. She relished in the feeling that he was frustrated even though she knew that every bit of the control she exercised in public would be paid for tenfold in private.

She thought about this one night as she lay in her bed after he had yet again and brutalized her that day. She thought about how sick she was and how twisted her thinking was. Why would anyone taunt an animal knowing it would bite? She came to the conclusion that the animal needed no provocation, he would bite regardless. She turned over nursing the arm he had twisted behind her back and found the patch of hair he had yanked out as she fought him. She picked it up and threw it to the floor and again counted the days to freedom.

At 14 she had tried to run away several times, but never made it very far. Her parents had loosened the floorboards in her room so that they squeaked notifying them if she tried to sneak out. She was trapped in her own home. It suddenly struck her that she had always been caught downstairs when she tried to leave. She figured The Mother really didn't care or really want to know what was going on *up*stairs.

Things were worse now that The Mother had gone back to school full-time. She was more abusive when she was home. The stress and tension on Meg became increasingly unbearable. The Older Brothers took advantage of The Mother's absence and distractions. They constantly picked away at Meg. They hadn't called her by her name in years, and instead they referred to her as "it" or "gross" and called her "dog" when they spoke to her directly instead of using her name.

The Mother would leave notes for Meg with a list of the work she expected her to do after school. There were no notes left for The Brothers. Meg came home tense and anxious. Frequently, she would cause a ruckus on the bus on the way home with the younger brother. Creating chaos had become her M.O., because she didn't know how to live in the quiet, and she could control the chaos by encouraging others to act out. Their behavior would draw the attention away from her. Later in life she would refer to this tactic for survival as her "midget theory".

One day Meg was in a particularly bad mood. The oldest brother had humiliated her again in front of a group of older boys. She was 15 now and he was 17, and a senior. A nice boy in his class had talked to her. She hadn't had any experience with "nice" boys. The "'Sam's" who talked to her or wanted to be around her weren't the nice ones. Over the last few years she had developed a mouth that was foul and mean, again, a means of protection to keep others away.

This day she was standing outside the band room after school waiting for it to be opened. She could hear the sharp yells and slaps of football practice going on in the distance. She was standing against the wall fussing with her book bag when a group of senior boys came down the hallway heading for the parking lot. The Brother was among them. They were talking and laughing. They stopped at the door and one of them, the nice boy, Mark, smiled that her and said "Hi. Are you waiting to get in? Is the door locked?" Meg smiled back, shy and nervous from the attention and The Brothers' threatening look. She shuffled her feet and told him she was. That was it. That was the extent of the conversation. The Brother laughed and said, "You are really scraping the bottom of the barrel this time buddy! Don't you know she's a whore?"

Mark's face turned bright red and he clearly didn't know what to do or say. The group laughed at Meg and asked her what she charged. The Brother spat out, "she's the worst kind! She gives it for free!" Mark frowned awkwardly at his feet and then walked away from the group, clearly uncomfortable. The others taunted her at the behest of The Brother. She felt humiliated and paralyzed. She sat down and tried to look busy with her book bag. She had no words, no reply; just seething anger and shame. Traitor tears tried to fall but she would not let them. She would not let anyone see her cry...ever. She berated herself inwardly, telling herself how stupid, how weak and how ugly she was.

As soon as they left, she thought of several things she could have said, things that would have exposed The Brother. Why couldn't she think of them at the time? Why was she so stupid? Look how weak you are! All you did was let him humiliate you! Just like at home! You just let him do those things to you! Are you really that stupid to believe that a nice boy would actually like you! You are poison! No wonder everyone treats like you are garbage! Remember your place, dog!

She caught the bus home early. On the bus ride home she made a decision. All the evidence was there. For as long as she could remember, she had no value. She was told consistently that she was stupid and would never amount to anything, that she was fat, ugly and a whore and that no one would want her. That she was nothing but a dog and a waste of space. She thought about it now with this latest humiliation and the group consensus from those boys. She accepted the "facts" as they were given. The decision was made and an action formed as she thought," okay then I can be that." Now resolved, she resolutely set herself on a path of self-destruction.

CHAPTER 9

THE MESS

Meg began getting in trouble in school. She was cutting classes, drinking and being generally obnoxious. She had decided she was going to make people see her. Before, she was seemingly invisible. Adults looked through her, over her. By lashing out now, she tried to force them to deal with her, to *see* her. She ended up being sent to the principal's office eight times that year for various infractions from punching people, mouthing off at the teachers, and drawing pictures of a teacher with a dagger blooming from his chest (that one she got paddled for!). In all of these encounters, no one ever asked her what was going on or why she was behaving this way. If her bruises and scars were invisible to everyone, she would make sure her presence was not. She came to believe that what her mother and brothers had always said was the truth. She was stupid and a waste of space and above all, she didn't matter in the grand scheme of things. She had seen how the two girls she'd beaten up after lunch were treated. They mattered, they were given tissues and were listened to and shown great care as they tearfully described the abuse they undeservedly suffered at the hands of that girl. No one had ever shown that kind of care for her when she suffered far worse at the hands of The Brothers and The Mother. It didn't matter that the reason she beat on those girls was because they had walked behind her and called her a slut and said she was ugly. She tried to explain that the others weren't innocent, but it all fell on deaf ears.

She took her latest writing assignment from the principal and walked out into the empty hallway and straight out the front door of the school. She walked down the street and kept walking. Headed down the road toward her house she silently and tearfully walked the 7 miles from the school through the fields and woods. The angry tears flowed down her face as she tried to understand what she did to deserve all the crap she endured. She was angry because she knew that when she got home she was going to be in trouble and probably whipped for being in trouble at school. That was a hard and fast rule The Mother had. If you get in trouble at school you'd better expect a whipping at home. The Mother was very consistent in her abuse, or punishment as she labeled it. It didn't matter *why* you did it, it mattered ***that*** you did it. To bring unwanted attention on her and on the family would never be tolerated. She couldn't have it look like The Mother was a bad parent, or that there were problems in the household. The Mother went to great lengths to ensure that what happened at home stayed at home. That was another hard and fast rule The Mother enforced consistently and violently.

The summer Meg turned 15 held great anticipation for her. The Brother was finally going away to college in the fall. She would gleefully listen to all the preparation and plans. He was going to go away and live in the dorms. He may or may not come home for holidays. Meg secretly wished the time would go faster. That summer The Brother was particularly brutal to Meg in physical beatings and poison words. She endured it clinging to the knowledge that her freedom was coming. The Brother would be gone soon. She believed it was worse now because he no longer had her at a total disadvantage. She fought back harder. She even got "mouthier" at him when he came after her. He could and would dominate her physically but she now would call him names. As he brutalized her she would call him pathetic and disgusting. He'd choked her by forcing her face into a pillow until she couldn't breathe, but when she could get a gulp of precious air she would use it to let fly a string of profanity and adjectives at him like they were flaming arrows, and he in turn would hurt her more.

The day finally arrived. The Brother's car was packed, the father's truck was full of The Brother's belongings. It was finally here... He was really going! She taunted him today as he packed his things, daring him to do something with the father there. She called him "big man". She was relentless right up until he left. She stood in the middle-of-the-road watching his car drive away. The sense of relief and freedom was nothing short of profound.

That night Meg went to her room after finishing the dishes. She had secretly waited for this. This was the first time she ever felt a sense of possible liberty. She went into her room and looked around. The room had no door. She had never really noticed it until now. The Mother had had it removed long ago. Meg had never been told why but she believed The Mother wanted her to know she had no rights or privacy. As if Meg had needed a reminder!

As she looked around, she quickly became aware that the room was not, nor ever would be, a sanctuary. It was still a cell, and always would be. The Brother may be gone, but his presence was still here. As her gaze alighted on each corner of her personal prison, it lingered somewhere, snagged sharply to the odd thing out. He had left her a parting gift. One of her stuffed dogs hung from her headboard with a wire hanger wrapped around his neck partially decapitating it. Its stuffing lay strewn across her pillow and bed in a flurry of sadness and pain.

She didn't react, she didn't cry, she wasn't afraid, she just... checked out. She went inside herself and curled up on the floor and went to sleep, defeated, just like under the tree so long ago.

Meg awoke to her mother hitting her and screaming at her. It took her a few minutes to realize where she was. It took a few more minutes for her mother's raging words to register in her mind. The Mother wanted to know why Meg would do such a sick and twisted thing. The Mother screamed vicious names at her. Meg dodged and weaved but wasn't able to fend off the blows. The Mother screamed at Meg, "Answer me! I said I want an answer!" every syllable reinforced with a slap and a punch. "Why did you do that?" The Mother yelled pointing to Meg's bed. Meg looked and saw the maimed stuffed dog hanging on her bed headboard. Meg finally understood what The Mother's problem was. Meg tried to speak but was met with the incessant slaps to the face, "I didn't! I didn't do it!" She finally managed to scream at The Mother. "He left it! He did it!"

The Mother became more enraged. "Don't you lie to me! He didn't have time to do something like that! He's not sick and twisted like that, I know you did it!" With that, a fresh barrage of hits ensued. "You are sick girl! You should be locked up!" The Mother grabbed the maimed stuffed dog and threw it from Meg's room. Meg stood very still in the silence, wondering if she would ever win or escape. She marveled at the beautifully terrible predictability of the process. The Brother perpetrates. Meg responds or doesn't. The Mother brutalizes and marginalizes Meg. Then silence. Somehow the silence was always the worst part, because in the silence, is the waiting - for the next outburst, the next attack, the next whatever. In the silence, she had time to think or contemplate or worse, feel. In the noise and activity she knew what to do - defend, evade, survive. In the silence, her thoughts, her mother's words, her memories, were all deafening. In the silence, she didn't know what to do, because there was nothing to react off of, nothing to define herself against. She cleaned up the remains of the stuffing on her bed with a blank expression. She felt nothing.

Over the next few weeks, during summer band practices, before school started, Meg was different. She had always been mouthy and loud, and now she was more so! She became lascivious and flirtatious, attention seeking in the worst places. She was just three months away from turning sixteen. She was a junior this year. Though The Brother was gone, she still felt cautious amidst her feelings of relief. She had survived. But she was not unscathed. She felt nothing and didn't realize the extent of how damaged she was. She had been prey for far too long and had vowed never to be a victim again. Now she was the predator. She flirted and teased and humiliated the boys around her. She felt nothing for herself or for them.

On her first day of school she walked down the hallway to her locker, assessing the environment for possible threats. She didn't realize that this is how she lived her life, anticipating danger and brutality and preparing for it. She reunited with the few friends that she had. She was overly boisterous and loud, almost giddy as she told her friends her pre-prepared lies of how great her summer had been and of all the amazing stories she had invented for herself. They knew she lied, but her storytelling was entertaining so they didn't care. When she lied, she felt above the sightline for once.

She went from class to class and through lunch relaxing a little more as the day wore on and no one messed with her. Most of the classes were easy, especially on day one of the school year. She now walked down the hallway toward the door she dreaded the most; geometry class. She hated math. Meg had wanted to enroll in the business classes but The Mother insisted she take the academic classes because she expected Meg to go to nursing school; the only time The Mother seemed to want to see any reflection of herself in her only daughter. It didn't matter that Meg desperately wanted to teach. The Mother had it all planned out.

Outside the classroom door stood the usual gaggle of loitering students waiting for the last possible second to enter the room. As she walked slowly toward the door, she saw him - how could she miss him! There standing in the group towering above them all, was The One. Meg's breath caught in her throat, and she felt as if she'd been knocked on her back.

Meg didn't understand what was happening to her. As she stood there she found herself staring at the tall, handsome, young man in front of her. She found herself transfixed, watching him. He wasn't doing anything remarkable (he didn't have to), just the sight of him standing there, looking so tall and strong sent butter-flies fluttering through her belly. It was a new feeling, and more importantly, it was *a* feeling - Meg had felt so numb to the world for so long now that it took her by surprise. She jumped when the bell rang and quickly entered the room and took her assigned seat. She continued to find herself a little breathless as she watched the tall young man enter the room and take his seat two rows over from her. As she sat through the class she found herself become increas-ingly nervous. She realized she couldn't wait to find an opportu-nity to talk to the young man even though she had no clue what she would say! As he sat in his chair she watched him, hoping he wouldn't catch her staring. She couldn't help but notice how dif-ficult it was for him to fold his massive frame into the tiny school desk. He had one chair in front of him and she noticed how he had to fidget and adjust to keep his long legs out of the aisle and into the space allotted. He looked uncomfortable and cramped and slightly perplexed. She noticed that he seemed to be nervous as well, and she vowed to find out what his story was. She began to wonder why she had never seen him or noticed him before, es-pecially considering his sasquatch like stature. She wondered if he was new here. Meg found herself so caught up in her musings about the young man that she almost leapt from her chair in alarm when the bell rang signaling the end of class. She gathered her books and school supplies quickly, hoping not to miss an opportunity to "bump" into him. She made it to the hallway first since her desk was strategically positioned adjacent to the door. She dawdled in the hallway acting as if she might have forgotten something in the room.

The young man came through the door swiftly and awkwardly, almost running into her in his haste to exit the room. There was no way he could avoid her now, as she was unintentionally blocking his path down the hallway. He looked down at her perplexed and apologized.

She looked up at him and smiled with a shy, giggles laugh and said, "Not a problem. Not a problem at all." His face flushed bright red as he looked nervously around looking for an escape. She found herself not knowing what to say, which was totally out of character for the person she had forced herself to become. He began to move away from her, heading down the hallway towards the exit. It took her a minute to realize that he was leaving. She composed herself, regrouped, and headed quickly after him.

"Hey! Are you okay?" She asked, touching his arm. Again, he flushed and looked around nervously.

" Yeah." And then silence. She noticed he had trouble looking her in the eyes. She began to wonder if maybe he had heard things about her, and if that was what was making him nervous. Suddenly, she became very self-conscious and her ugly friend, that familiar self-defeating shame, tapped again on her shoulder. Now *she* was nervous as she stood there berating herself for being so stupid.

"Okay, then." Meg asked him his name and told him hers. He didn't say much and she realized how hard it was to have a conversation when only one person was talking. She took it to mean that he wasn't interested (how could anyone be interested in someone as pathetic as her), which made her sadder than she would have thought possible. It was indescribable and incomprehensible to her that she would feel that way, that she would feel anything at all, but she did.

"Well I guess I'll see you in class. It was nice to meet you." She said as she began to back away from him. He just nodded looking relieved that she was moving away.

The rest of her school day passed in a haze. Nothing could keep her attention. All she could think about was the young man; how it felt to stand near him, how blue his eyes were, how tall and handsome he was. She had never felt anything like this before. She began to wonder what he liked, where he lived, did he have a girlfriend, was he looking for a girlfriend? The more she thought about him, the more questions came to mind and the more she wanted to know about him. And again, like before, the self-defeating talk began inside her head. "Even if he does want a girlfriend, what makes you think he would have anything to do with you? Don't forget your place, dog! He seems like a nice boy, nice boys will never like you, remember? You are ruined after what Sam and The Brother did to you. Just forget it, you'll never be good enough for him or anyone."

As soon as it began, she felt the weight of those words begin to take their usual effect. She felt the heaviness, the defeat, the rejection. She began to feel very glad that no one had seemed to see her talking to him. At least she would be spared some humiliation, and could save him from the stigma of having been seen with her.

By the time she boarded the bus home she was in a foul mood. She waited until the ride was nearly over and, as usual, picked a fight with the younger brother, guaranteeing that any scrutiny from The Mother would be about bus etiquette and behavior, thus preventing any possible conversation that may lead to less desirable topics. Sure enough and true to form the younger brother told The Mother all Meg had done to him on the bus, the ruckus which had ensued and the inevitable yelling and hitting and finally, banishment to her room for the night. Mission accomplished. She would probably be left alone for the remainder of the evening. The Mother, Meg had learned over the years, wasn't very creative when it came to her parenting abilities, but at least she was nothing if not predictable.

Meg used her solitary confinement to her advantage. She sneaked into the Older Brother's room and snatched last year's Yearbook. The middle brother had always been The Mother s favorite, and he got all the good stuff. HE, she spent money on. HE, she doted on. HE, could do no wrong and HE, knew it and HE used it. He was the male version of The Mother. Though he rarely hit Meg but he regularly humiliated her. It was his yearbook she now held in her hands. She knew she had to be stealthy because if the middle brother found out she was interested in a boy he would do anything and everything to humiliate her and Alan. The middle brother did with his mouth what the oldest brother did with his fists. He would taunt and strike with his words, violating her in every way. He was the golden boy, good looking, The Mother's favorite, the captain of the football team and the worst part was his intelligence equaled his spite towards her and her younger brother. He frequently took part in the torture and humiliation of Meg with the oldest brother while The Mother was at school or work. He was a master of public humiliation of not just Meg, but anyone he felt he could get away with it. He took all of his own insecurity, hurt and pain and transferred it to whoever stood in firing range. That made him popular among the jock crowd. Meg had tried out for cheerleading that summer because The Mother had been a cheerleader and pushed Meg to try out, though simultaneously berated her about her lack of beauty, talent, or coordination.

Meg went to the first practice and stood in the hallway with the squad she was assigned to, practicing the moves they just learned. The middle brother and other members of the football team came down the hallway skipping and singing a dirty limerick. As they skipped through the hallway singing their disgusting song, they had come to a stop in front of Meg. The middle brother looked at the other girls standing in a row beside her and said, "This one's for you Sis!" and then began singing "How much is that doggy in the window? The one that is destined to fail? Arf, Arf!" Everyone, including Megs' friends beside her, began to laugh and at the appropriate time in the song sang, "Arf! Arf!" along with the rest of the jocks. The Middle Brother began to skip and dance around her along with the other boys, entreating the cheerleaders to join in. This time the traitor tears would not be stopped. She picked up her duffel bag and left the building. Again she started the 7 mile walk home with tears streaming down her face. That night she relived the humiliation as the Middle Brother told The Mother of Megs' inability to "take a joke." How she walked out crying like a baby. The Mother laughed at Meg and told her she better toughen up. There would be no criers in her family, The Mother reiterated, or apologies, as both were signs of weakness (which she learned from John Wayne, apparently). She fed the middle brother extra dessert as a sign of her pride in him. Meg was told she was already too fat.

"No," she thought, "he, nor The Mother can ever find out that I am interested in any boy."

CHAPTER 10

REMEMBRANCES

M eg sat there alone on the loveseat drinking her hot cocoa and enjoying the warmth of the fire in the fireplace. It had been a long time since she had had a leisurely moment to herself to think about anything.

She didn't think of her childhood often. At 45 a lot of time had passed since those days; a lifetime.

Her husband would be home soon. It was always her favorite part of the day, the evenings with him. She still found it unfathomable that this man that she loved with all of her being seemed to love her that much as well.

Her thoughts drifted back to that day in the hallway of the school, the day they met. Who would've ever guessed that the two of them; the shy, tall, beautiful boy, and the damaged, broken girl; would build a life with such wonder and adventure? She laughed a little at that. It certainly had been an adventure! For that she turned her thoughts to the Lord and His part in all of it for which she and her husband were truly grateful.

She was fifteen that day in that hallway almost thirty years ago. He was sixteen. Her thoughts began to drift through time.

Their first date, which was a week or two after they met, she had had to ask him out! They had gone to a football game and then to a friend's party. Their first movie date, and a week later, their first kiss. They were inseparable. They spent all the time they could steal at school together. With him, she found the only happiness she had ever known.

She thought back to the first time they made love and the times after that, resulting in the birth of their first child when she was only 16. It had all changed after that.

The Mother and father were cruel about it all, as were The Brothers. The Middle Brother had gotten his girlfriend pregnant at the same time. He used Meg as his "midget" with The Mother. He continuously threw her under the bus when the tension rose. He reminded The Mother that he was taking care of his responsibility by marrying his girlfriend and going into the military when The Mother began tirades - the first time, it seemed, anyone had been on the receiving end of that rod besides for Meg.

Upon hearing the news of her pregnancy from The Mother, the father told Meg that she wasn't worth feeding. The few times in her life that she could recall the father talking to her directly added much more weight and significance to his words that day. They were harsh and final. He had said them with a disgust in his eyes that matched his words. She had no doubt that he meant what he said, as he always did when he chose to speak, times which were few and far between. She believed him, and the words entwined themselves into her very being, her demeanor and her heart. She was no good and should have never been born. This time though, there was another being to protect, something whose life did have value.

Meg enjoyed the pregnancy. Alan graduated that year and made plans for school in the fall. She still had another year of high school and was determined to finish; her baby wasn't due until the fall. She spent a lot of time with Alan through the summer, for which she was grateful. The Older Brother had come home from college for the summer and mercilessly badgered her. He did hit her several times. This time was different. She informed The Mother and The Brother that she was being examined by a doctor and she would make sure that he knew exactly where the bruises were coming from; and that now, Alan would also know. She was done keeping the secrets of their abuse.

The Mother, not one to be threatened, stated, "Go ahead. Do you think he will believe you after I talk to him?" Meg understood very well what The Mother would do. She would make up whatever needed to be made up to keep Meg in check.

Nevertheless, the Older Brother didn't hit her much after that, but his words were just as damaging. She did what she could to stay out of the house while he was there.

She sat on the loveseat remembering the stress of those days. It had been a long, hot summer that year. She had worked at home taking care of the house and enduring The Mother's rage directed towards her. The Middle Brother had gotten married that May and was now gone in the military. The Mother was not happy to have her golden boy gone. As a result of his absence, her mood was fouler than usual, and Meg took the brunt of the anguish. The youngest brother, now twelve, stayed outside most of the day playing with friends, especially when the Older Brother was home. The younger brother was now a prime target for all the rage he could no longer direct towards Meg.

Meg went with Alan to move his things into the boarding house where he would be staying during the 18 month school he was attending to become an electrician. The school was 80 miles from her home and she knew it would not be possible to see him during the week. It may as well have been 800 miles. They had talked about the separation and he pledged to come home every weekend and be with her. They talked about their future. He had asked her father for permission to marry her, to which he got a "grunt" in reply. Alan took it as a yes and bought her a small diamond ring.

Alan remained true to his word. He came home every weekend to be with her. Her weeks were miserable without him. She was a Senior now, but could not, nor did she want to, participate in all of the Senior year reverie. She just wanted to be with him and get out on her own - to be with the first person who had ever truly made her feel safe.

The two Older Brothers were both gone now, one back to college and the other in the military. She envied them their freedom from The Mother, and she longed for her own day of escape. The Mother was cruel as ever to Meg, filling her head with scenarios about the distance Alan was from her, and how he was most assuredly meeting other girls and having a great time without her. She would tell Meg that he would not be there for her long term because he was a man, after all, and now that he had gotten it from her he was almost definitely looking for someone to give it to him where he was now because he wasn't going to go without it. She told her that she needed to get used to being left alone and that she needed to take care of herself because no one was going to want her and a kid, and he would be moving on to someone respectable.

Meg tried to hold onto what she knew of Alan. He had been there so far and had kept true to his word. Her words were constant and relentless. Meg would often talk to Alan about The Mother's beliefs, and it made her feel clingy, because now that she had experienced true love and comfort it was anguish to live without it. She could see and feel the stress between them. She was overly emotional and he was overwhelmed with all of it. The responsibility of becoming a father and a husband, the demands of school and being away, and the pressure from his own family to leave Meg were taking their toll.

His mother and sisters made no secret of the fact that they didn't approve of Meg from the beginning. Meg didn't know what she had done wrong and didn't understand at first. It became something she just accepted over time because she believed that they thought she was bad for Sam, and as she believed that to be true about herself, she felt she couldn't blame them. It made it very difficult for Alan. Every family event she attended with him was filled with tension and trauma, usually ending with Meg being hurt and him defending his family, justifying and explaining that what his mother or sisters said wasn't meant to be hurtful. Meg knew different but Alan was good - down to depth of his soul good - and he truly believed that they didn't mean anything hurtful. It became a continuous stress between them.

Meg didn't feel safe anywhere, and now she was bringing a child into the mix. Her world was so filled with conflict and pain. Even the one relationship she had that meant everything to her was being tainted by her inability to be normal. As the months progressed toward the impending birth, Meg thought more and more about what she wanted for herself and her child.

She knew she didn't want to become like The Mother, but she didn't know how not to. She had never experienced anything else. Meg had her anger and mouth. She could be cruel and petty. Her time with Alan had been the only thing to begin warming her inside, but had it been enough time? Had it been enough love to begin unwinding the webs of hurt, the terror, the pain she had experienced? Had she been hardened too far, had she really turned to stone? She had felt something strong for Alan, and it was like nothing she had ever experienced before. It was like she came alive when she met him. He was the one good thing in a world where she was all wrong. And now they were having a baby together and she was so afraid that she was dooming her child, his child, to a life like her own. He was good and she was not. Would this child be tainted just by association? Would the child's goodness be like its father's? Meg could only hope, but hope was not something Meg knew too much about. It was too much for her to think about, so she mentally checked out when she was alone. She was back to the numbness during the week, just existing until he would come home for the weekend. Now though, they mostly had awful fights due to her emotional upheaval from pregnancy and The Mother's "he's cheating because he's a man" mantra. There was nothing he could say that would reassure her that he loved her and that he would not abandon her. She felt as if she were truly losing herself and her mind, and she didn't know what to do. She felt like the walls were closing in on her, and there was nowhere to turn for help. She saw the small light of joy she had found so briefly begin to slip away from her again.

CHAPTER 11

SURVIVAL

Meg stood and went into the kitchen and deposited her mug in the sink. It was hard to think about that time. Now, from where she stood in life and with all the things in between, she could look back at the Meg she had been and love her for where she had been. She smiled ruefully to herself as she thought of how the girl she had been would respond to her having love for her. Let's just say the response wouldn't be warm and fuzzy!

She had survived it all. She hadn't done it all well, but she had done it. She thought about her children as she looked at a family picture just recently taken. How grateful she is, even for the pain.

She had inevitably given birth to her first child at sixteen, and Alan was there with her. He never left her side as their Sara made her way into the world and into their hearts. When Meg held her child for the first time, she resolved some things right there. She would not be like The Mother, she would raise a strong woman, one that felt safe and secure and supported. She would do whatever she needed to do to help her reach her potential and she would be good like Alan. They would be good together.

She knew it would not be easy, but what was ever easy for her. She also had doubts as to whether she could do it. Nonetheless, she was determined.

Four weeks later Meg was back in school determined to finish her senior year. She wanted to go to school in the fall. She had always wanted to become a teacher. History was her favorite subject. The Mother had other plans for her. The Mother had determined that Meg needed to go to nursing school so that if Alan left her, as The Mother determined he would, she would be able to take care of herself and her child. Meg did not want to become a nurse but The Mother's insistence was never anything Meg could get around.

Three months later everything changed. The Mother and the father decided to move to another part of the country and Meg was not given any choice in the matter. She was forced to go. The fact that she was only seventeen meant that The Mother and the father still held decision-making power over her and her infant child.

There wasn't much time between the time that she was notified that they would be leaving and the time they actually left. It was a matter of weeks. Meg was absolutely distraught. She was only allowed to take the few belongings that her Sara had and very few belongings that she had. Decisions had to be made for space allowed. Meg ended up leaving behind most of her precious things in favor of necessities.

Meg and Alan had a very difficult time trying to figure out how to make this work over long distance. They would be separated by more than 1000 miles and to them at that time, it may well have been the distance from the Earth to the moon. Alan had to finish school, but he would be done in June. Meg still had to finish high school and she would be done in May. Their separation was imminent and it was only February.

Meg had begged The Mother and the father to allow her to stay and finish school here, but they would not listen. Others came forward to offer their home for Meg and her child so she could finish her school in the same place. The Mother would hear none of it.

The father had left on a plane the week before and now it was time for Meg, The Mother, The Younger Brother and Sara to make the long trip in the car. The car was packed to the roof with possessions, but all Meg cared about was Sara and the empty space where Alan should have been. There was barely any room for Meg or the baby to sit. It was not a comfortable trip.

It would take more than 24 hours for them to complete the journey from beginning to end. Meg had a lot of time to think. She dared not cry - The Mother would have none of that either. Meg missed Alan terribly already. She stared wondering what their future held. Would he wait for her? Would he find another, like The Mother had anticipated? Meg had her suspicions that The Mother wasn't merely anticipating it, but hoping for it. Grief and anger overwhelmed her.

Meg focused on the infant Sara. She busied herself trying to make her comfortable. When The Mother or the younger brother tried to speak to Meg, she answered only in monosyllables or grunts. "Just like my daddy." She thought snidely. She had learned nothing else from him. Her lack of communication caused The Mother much irritation. Meg secretly rejoiced.

The journey ended at about 1200 miles from her previous home. It was hot and dry and there was no real grass, just brown sand and brown trees and brown everything. She had come from green forests and green lush grass to what looked like a burnt barren wasteland with a Cul de Sac. She marveled at the change. She was going to live here?! This only added to the raging fire of anger already burning strong in her gut, and her determination to make her own decisions as soon as she could. Soon anger was going to be her constant companion and color her whole world.

CHAPTER 12
SURVIVING

M eg settled into a routine. She determinedly attended school during the day even though the school didn't have the same classes that she had been enrolled in up north. They ended up placing her in classes that she had taken in the ninth grade, and told her she only really needed to show up for home room attendance as she had more than enough credits to graduate.

The Mother arranged a job for her at a fast food restaurant after school through the late evening, leaving Meg very little time to see her Sara or do homework. Meg wondered if this was on purpose, as The Mother frequently accused Meg of not caring about her Sara or of The Mother's burden of having to take care of the child so that Meg could finish high school. Meg noticed that The Mother's interference with Meg's schedule provided The Mother with ample time to play mommy to Sara, and that The Mother seemed to covet the role. Meg's anger increased with every accusation that she didn't care for her child, and with every wedge The Mother tried to drive between Meg and her baby. Meg confessed inwardly that she didn't know what she was doing with the baby. She had had no instruction from The Mother, just more yelling and derision. The Mother would make fun of her for how she held the baby or what she dressed her in or the way she talked to the baby. There was never anything helpful or instructive, only criticism and mocking which usually ended with The Mother taking the child from Meg and yelling at her to do some work.

Meg would go do the work, seething. Traitor tears from anger would be quickly wiped away so the mother couldn't use them as ammunition against Meg. She would not give her that satisfaction. As she worked, she would think about getting away. She would focus on the time left in the school year until she could graduate. She was beginning to suspect that The Mother would do something to keep her here, or at least keep the baby. She shuddered. She would never let that happen. She resolved to do whatever she had to do to get through it and get out. In the back of her mind though as always, she believed The Mother was right, that she was not good for the baby because she didn't know what to do or how to be a mom.

Two months. It had been two months since she had heard from Alan. The Mother was downright giddy and gloating when she would come back from the mailbox and there would be no letter yet again. She would make the same remark. "Guess he's too busy with someone else to care about you. I told you, men cheat. They use you then leave you."

Meg couldn't take it today. She looked at The Mother and said, "So was this the plan all along? Move me here to prove to me that he isn't coming back or was it to make sure he wouldn't? Did you do it so that you could play mommy and keep punishing me? Is that why you make me work late at night too so that I can't be here? Who does that? Who gloats and is happy when their own child is hurt? Selfish, ignorant, sick people that's who! That's you!"

A cloud descended over The Mother's face. Meg knew it well. She had done it now. The Mother didn't hesitate she came at her like a bull and with every ugly word and syllable she beat Meg with her fists. Meg didn't move this time or try to evade. Instead, she welcomed the blows. She'd earned them. The Mother was seething and spit her hateful words at Meg. The baby was crying now. Meg pushed The Mother out of her way and went to the infant. The Mother tried to pry the baby out of Meg's hands but Meg's grip held. The Mother furiously grabbed Meg by the hair and yanked her head in different directions. Meg could feel her hair coming out at the roots but held her ground. "Not much longer. Just hold on!" she thought. Soon the father would be home and The Mother would not want him to see her thus engaged. The Mother would put on a scene for him, to let him know how she had been disrespected and mistreated. She would tell him how she had to "cuff her up" to get Meg to comply but minimize her brutality and not mention the vile words and ugly things that accompanied the "cuffing".

The Mother realized the time at some point and let her go, telling her to get out of her sight, which Meg knew meant not to be seen directly when the father got home. The Mother needed the time to set the stage for her performance, get her props together and to be properly ensconced in a chair. She had to prepare the right countenance as well. Would she play the martyr? Maybe the indignant, put upon heroine....or would she be the angry, self–righteous defender of all things holy?

In the end The Mother chose martyrdom. After everything she has done for Meg and after what Meg had put her through, how could Meg possibly treat her so horribly and disrespectfully? Meg listened from her room as The Mother went on and on about how her high crimes and misdemeanors had caused the fall of civilization as we know it.

Meg laughed snidely to herself. "I **wish** I had that kind of power." she thought. When she had heard enough and the baby was now in need of a bottle, she left her room and headed silently through the living room to the kitchen. She looked straight ahead and didn't stop when her mother spit a rhetorical question at her from her perch. "Why do you keep doing these things? I have done everything for you and this is how you treat me?"

Meg reached the refrigerator and sighed as she began to heat a bottle. The Mother still hadn't stopped talking by the time the bottle was ready. Meg made her way back to her room and shut the door in silence. She sat down on the bed and fed and rocked her baby girl. She could really feel the pain now from where The Mother had hit her and from her scalp where her hair had been uprooted. When the baby was asleep she would go to the bathroom and survey the damage. In the meantime, she listened to the sound of her infant feeding, and stared into her angelic face wishing she could feel something other than sadness and anger.

Maybe everyone was right, maybe she was too damaged to be a person let alone a mom. Obviously no one wanted her. Alan was not in contact with her, The Brothers reminded her verbally and physically of her general worthlessness and would tell of her specific unworthiness to anyone who would listen, The Mother had never wanted her and the father had told her she wasn't worth feeding.

She stared at her Sara's face. She looked so small and peaceful. Some of The Mother's words intruded into her thoughts. "You won't ever be able to take care of that baby! You don't even have enough sense to dress her properly! You wouldn't do anything unless I told you to, she would be laying around in filth and dirt if it wasn't't for me!"

"Filth and dirt." she thought. All of the sudden an overwhelming sense of guilt and shame washed over her. She looked at her infant in her arms and felt as if her very presence defiled the babe in some way. She looked around the little room taking note of the overfull laundry basket and the cluttered area near the door where her school stuff laid on the floor. She made a note of the fact that she hadn't vacuumed in here in a week, and that her bed was still unmade and had been for some time.

Was The Mother right? Meg would surely take care of those things if The Mother had told her to, but left on her own she hadn't even noticed any of it. She would get no credit for anything she had done as long as The Mother had told her to do it and even then it would be viewed as something expected.

Even through her anger, the feelings hit her like a freight train. She felt…..need. She needed. She wanted and needed The Mother and father's approval. The tears came fast and hot down her cheeks. She was overwhelmed and bewildered. Confusion overtook her as she warred within herself. The Mother couldn't be right could she? After all, Alan had left her.

Anger made itself known again. "Be careful what you wish for, you just might get it. You wanted to feel something and it don't feel good."

CHAPTER 13

ENOUGH

Something was wrong. She could sense it as soon as she entered the house. She had just finished her shift at the restaurant and it was late. She had had to close again tonight. Thank goodness there were only two more weeks of school.

"Where have you been?" The Mother asked from the darkened living room.

"At work. I had to close again." Meg answered.

"You're a liar. They just called here for you and said you didn't finish your work and wanted you come back in. Where were you?"

Meg stood there dumbfounded trying to figure out what was happening. What did she forget to do? She headed back toward the door.

"I asked you where you were! It's a boy isn't it? You are out running around with some boy while I'm here taking care of your kid! Who were you with? You'll never change! Still a whore!" The Mother said as she moved toward Meg.

Anger overthrew every other emotion. Meg headed for the door to go back into work. She whirled around to face The Mother and spit out, "Just for the record, nothing you said is anywhere near the truth but I'll tell you what, mother, you have called me that for a very long time and it has not been true but I will not force you to lie anymore!"

Meg watched The Mother's face in the dim light and shadow of the darkened room. She wondered later if she imagined or could trust what she thought she saw there. She could have sworn that what she saw could only be described as satisfaction. She had a strange gleam in her eyes and a lunatic smile on her face like she was....happy.

Over the next month The Mother watched Meg closely. Meg, irritated by The Mother's diligence, began to do things to be provocative. She had started accepting invitations to dates with friends and with boys. Her anger at Alan and her mother made her feel as if she had the right to act up. She answered none of The Mother's baited questions. Meg had given up in her heart that Alan was going to contact her, and The Mother was only too happy to reaffirm it as fact as still no word had come.

Meg had given up on a lot of things at this point. The Oldest Brother had shown up in the middle of the night three days ago now. He had dropped out of college with two weeks left in the semester because something happened with a girl. Meg wasn't privy to the details but she knew it wasn't good. He had started in on her right away. It felt like he picked up where he left off with his berating and abuse. The Mother was only too happy to fill him in on Meg's latest shortcomings and failures to add fuel to his fire. Together they were experts at destroying another human being. If it were an Olympic event they would be the gold medal winners. Like putty in their hands Meg acted out, acted up and self-destructed.

CHAPTER 14

TOO MUCH

S he couldn't breathe. Was she even conscious? She took a minute to register her surroundings. Yep she was awake - and then
wished she wasn't.

She lay there listening to hear if her attacker were still around.
She moved slowly, rolling to her left side trying not to hiss at the
pain. She heard nothing except the sound of her own heartbeat
in her ears and her shallow breaths.

What had she done?

The Mother and father and the Older Brother had left two days
earlier to go back to their old home in the North with her Sara to
take care of the sale of their old house. Meg had to stay behind
to work and go to school. In all of herself destructive behavior
she still managed to keep a job and good GPA. She had been
hanging out with an unsavory lot as well as drinking and being
generally obnoxious. Her "I can be that" statement was beginning
to become a bit of a reality. She was sure The Mother would be
secretly pleased if she were aware of Meg's activities. She didn't
feel or need anymore. She was numb again, worse than before.

She thought there was no coming back from this one so she threw herself into the abyss.

She sat up on the floor and peeked around. She was sure she was alone now. Had it really happened? She looked down at herself. She was naked from the waist down and could see the dried blood on her thighs. Her shirt was torn at the top but not all the way down. She pulled up her bra to cover her breasts and pulled the shirt off and put it on backwards to cover herself. She looked around and found first her pants but never found her panties. He must have taken them. The thought made her shudder at first and then made her angry. Anger, her longtime faithful companion was never far away and was always consistent. Anger made her move, it motivated her, it kept her going. It began to burn as she began to put together the pieces of what had happened here.

"You're coming right? It's the last one of our Senior year. Come on, you gotta come to one!" Devon said.

"Yeah. It better be good though. I've waited a long time. Where is it again?" Meg asked. "I am free for the first time in months. I mean I have a whole week by myself. I still have to work though so I can't get too out of control."

"It's cool. We will have you home before you turn into a pumpkin Cinderella!!!" Devon replied laughing. "You know what they say, all work and no play...."

"Yeah, yeah. I have a kid I can't play too much. Although I have been making up for lost time the last few weeks!" Meg said.

By all appearances, she seemed to be engaging with the people around her now. The truth was that she was still numb. She could be here or at work or anywhere and it was all the same gray world. She had been suffering from nightmares since she was a little girl but now they were way worse since the Older Brother had moved home. She was having flashbacks again too. She hated them. They always came at the worst times, too. They came when she was awake. Waking and sleeping blurred together in a torturous haze. At school and at work she tried to contain them when they came, but people were noticing and giving her the "that chick's crazy" look. She felt crazy too. She found herself on edge all the time, constantly looking around for someone to hurt her. She wasn't sleeping much again either. Since she was little, she only slept maybe 2-3 hours at a time, then she would be up for hours and then fall asleep for another hour or two. It left her edgy. She always seemed to have energy though. It wasn't good energy though; she felt like a convict being chased by hounds. She felt like an alien most of the time around the normal people. She just couldn't relate so she used humor and sarcasm to create a shield for herself.

"So...what do you say? You're going right?" Devon asked snapping his fingers in front of her face.

"Yeah, I don't know, if I don't have to work. Where did you say it was again?" she asked again.

"At the Foundry. I will take you. You'll never find it by yourself. You get lost in the locker room I hear!" Devon said laughing.

Meg shook her head. She wasn't laughing. The incident he was referring to was a painful one. He didn't know that, no one did. She was caught in a flashback/blackout. When they happen they are so intense that she feels like she's completely experiencing the event again, and her body responds to the thing like it's being hit or kicked, just like it did when the original trauma happened.

She had been in the locker room, and some of Megs' friends had been taunting another girl. One of them had hit a locker and screamed in the other girls face and that was it. She was down the rabbit hole. She had ended up in the corner of one of the shower stalls fully clothed holding off two teachers with her fists yelling "I can't find the door! I can't get out!! Don't touch me!" The sound snapped her back to the time when her brothers locked her in a dark shed as a child. They had pounded on the outside of the shed and screamed at her until they got bored, and then finally left her there.

She shuddered and looked at Devon and said, "I'll let you know."

She hadn't gone to the foundry. She had stayed home drinking Bacardi and Coke's by herself. She had decided she didn't mind being alone and she didn't want to be Cinderella at the ball. The last thing she needed was a Prince Charming. She had thought Devon might be interested, but dismissed the notion as quickly as it had come. No one really wanted her. The Bacardi was doing its job - depression and self-pity were arriving right on schedule! Hopefully sleep or coma were next, she mused. At least she might get one night's decent sleep before the nightmare of reality came crashing home in 3 days. She missed her baby though. She was angry that The Mother took her with them. The Mother acted like she had every right to do whatever she pleased with Meg's baby. She didn't even ask, she just did it! And there you are old friend - anger had arrived at the party just in time. She preferred anger to depression. Anger had a cadence and could keep a beat. Anger was her hurt with a voice, and it spoke loudly. Anger wasn't afraid of anything.

At some point she must have passed out. She remembered waking to the sound of someone calling her name. The voice was familiar but she couldn't place it right away. She moved slowly to the door of her room and peeked out.

"Great. Busted!" she thought. It was the Neighbor's brother. He was much older than her but much younger than the Neighbor. The Neighbor must have sent him to check on her. She thought if she stayed quiet and very still he would think she was at work and leave. No such luck.

"Hey watcha doin in there honey? He asked. She could smell that he had been drinking too.

Meg opened the door and moved past him fast down the hallway to the front room near the main door.

"Nothin. I am kinda in the middle of something and I uh, need you to leave. My parents would not think it was cool for you to be here this late." Meg said firmly. This guy had always given her the creeps.

"Oh, oh…you've been drinkin'!" he said, smiling and shaking his finger at her. "How old are you darlin? 18?" he asked stepping closer.

"17. What do you want? Just call whoever sent you and tell them you busted me already." Meg said. She didn't like him getting close to her and she didn't like the way he was looking at her.

"Well now, I could do that and get you in trouble and all but I think there might be a better way to work this out. No harm's been done." He said leering, stepping closer.

"Who sent you to check on me? You better get back to them before they come looking for you too." she said hoping to get him to move back.

"Now about that, well I came over on my own. No one sent me. I was just talking to my sister this morning and she told me about your parents being out of town and you being here all by yourself and how worried she was about you being safe and all. She wasn't too worried because she said that she has seen how well you handle yourself around your brother and your mother."

Two things became very clear at the same time. One, that his sister had seen The Mother's and brother's abuse of her and Two, that he knew there was no one who would care if he hurt her too.

Fear gripped her gut and she began to back away toward the door. She misjudged where the coffee table was and ended up falling over it. She tried to crawl backwards but he was on her then. He had his hands over her mouth and was holding her by the hair.

"How do they all know how to do that? Is there like a school for abusers or something?" she thought wildly.

He dragged her back to the farthest back bedroom and threw her on the floor. He told her that if she screamed or told anyone, he would come for her and for her baby, no matter how long it took. He said he was a very patient man and that he had waited for this from the first time he met her 4 months ago.

"Opportunity always comes around to the patient man. It's like a rule or law or something." He said. "See no one's gonna care what happens here tonight. You and me we are the invisible. People see through us or past us like we're furniture. People expect bad things to happen to us because we exist to be used like furniture. Tonight you are gonna be my bed."

He had taken no care or pity on her. He was brutal and thorough in his violation of Meg. As she looked at herself and saw the dried blood on her thighs and felt the sticky goo he had left behind on her and in her, she was transported back to her penny tree all those years ago.

Meg sat there for an unknown period of time in limbo between reality and memory. Her body responded to both. She shook and cried and writhed in pain and anguish through every flashback feeling it all fresh. From moment to moment she felt herself slipping away. Somewhere in the back of her mind she knew there was something she must do but she just couldn't grasp what it was. It was important she knew but she couldn't reach it inside herself.

At one point she could hear The Mother's voice. She ran toward it, falling down, getting back up, running, running until she made it to the house. Inside now, there's The Mother, wait she's angry, wait, she has the belt....

Anger awoke her. Anger stood up and took control. Anger got her to move and reminded her what she needed to do.

With rage she stood up and ripped the shirt from her body and stomped to the bathroom. Just like The Mother had done once so long ago, she ran the water in the tub. It was hot. It stung the sore and torn flesh. She scrubbed herself mercilessly just as The Mother had done before. When she was done she dried herself roughly just like The Mother had done before. She took her soiled and shredded clothes and put them in the trash just like The Mother had done before. She got dressed and made herself a cup of cocoa and sat in the chair. Then she held herself and cried and cried just like she had done before.

CHAPTER 15

PLANS

M eg did her best to act normal. She went to work and school as normal. Her baby came home three days later and Meg threw herself into caring for her. The Mother was as vexing as ever, complaining about the state the house had degenerated to in her absence, calling Meg lazy and good for nothing. Meg didn't register the remarks or the complaints. She was living moment to moment, focused on her Sara and the last days of school. Graduation was coming, and she had plans. She was going to get an apartment, and enroll in the Junior College. She had looked into the single mother program and found that she could get financial aid and living expenses and child care while working part time at the school between classes. She had also looked into joining the ROTC program for the Air Force. She wasn't going to stay in that house one minute longer than she needed to. She was going to become a teacher. She knew it would be hard but she also knew she had to do it. She had never told anyone about the plan, especially The Mother. She was afraid The Mother would try to find some way to stop her, or steal Sara away from her. She knew The Mother would not be happy about her reaching out and taking her independence.

The letter came that afternoon. Alan finally wrote, apologizing for not writing more frequently or sooner. His family had tried to convince him that Meg and the baby would be better off and just fine without him. He had been confused for a while but he loved her and wanted her and his baby to be together - if there was still a chance. He had seen the baby when The Mother was up north and it made him realize how much he wanted and needed to be a part of Sara's life, and Meg's as well. Would she please talk to him? Could he call her on Saturday? Was it too late?

Meg finished reading the letter for the third time, holding it in her fingers like the most fragile of treasures. The Mother was pacing. She was putting great effort into masking her poorly concealed fury. She hadn't anticipated this.

"What's he got to say after all this time? You know you can't trust anything he says. He has already shown that he can't be trusted, that he will walk away and leave when it suits him. I took the baby over there out of courtesy because they knew we were there with her and I wasn't going to be accused of not letting them see her. He's the one who abandoned his child."

"Interesting," Meg thought, "I am not even in the equation, even now in her mind. She expected him to abandon me all along, so the crime isn't that he left me alone with a child, it's that he didn't see or inquire about his child. I am furniture." She shuddered.

Numbness was reigning tonight. It took note of the fact that The Mother was nervous though.

An outside force that she can't control is looming on the horizon and it has her edgy. That alone is reason enough to take the phone call tomorrow night. She thought snidely.

Meg folded the letter and put it back in the envelope, picked up her baby, and headed for her room.

"What did he say? Don't tell me he wants you back. I don't believe it." The Mother squealed from the kitchen. Meg didn't't answer as she continued walking evenly to her room, and shut the door.

The next night at the appointed hour, Meg sat indifferently in the living room with her baby in her lap. She was fussy tonight, probably because of the palpable stress emanating from The Mother. She wasn't good with things she couldn't control or manipulate.

At 7:10 the phone rang and The Mother jumped up to get it before Meg could even move. The Mother was grumbling about him being late right before she answered with a cheery "hello". Meg always referred to it as The Mother's Jane Jetson phony telephony voice. She could be beating you with something and still answer the phone with a pleasant "hello". She had spent her whole life practicing the best ways to hide the monster within the house, to present the perfect housewife without.

Meg sat still, waiting for The Mother to relinquish the phone. It would do no good to do anything else. The Mother in her practiced phony telephony voice sounded genuinely happy to "finally" hear from him and how is your dear mother etc. etc. etc.

"I suppose you want to talk to her. Well she's right here which surprises me because this is the first I've seen of her in a month of Sundays. I never know where she is or what she's doing. She brings home a paycheck so I know she's at least working and she is graduating so I know she's going to school. Other than that I got no clue. Oh yeah, here she is."

Numbness shifted a little as anger peeked through but remained silent. Meg moved to the phone alcove and sat down. The Mother reached for the baby but Meg held fast to her infant. The Mother walked away in a huff and took up pacing as she had the night before.

"Hello?" her voice sounded dead even in her own ears. She dared not let hope even come near.

"Hey," Alan said hesitantly. "How are you?"

At the first sound of his voice her insides leapt. What was that? She didn't know. She dare not explore it now.

"I'm fine, we're fine, the baby I mean, she's fine." she replied clumsily.

"It's good to hear your voice." Careful now.

Her insides leapt again. Why is it doing that? She thought irritated.

"Oh well it's the same old voice as before. You sound good. I guess you have been busy with school and whatever. Of course, I wouldn't know since we kinda lost touch there for a minute." she said, irritation clear in her voice. She looked at The Mother who was showing pleasure at Meg's obvious rancor.

At that Anger came forward. Not toward Alan but toward the Mother.

"Look. I'm really sorry and I'm glad that you are even talking to me right now. I want you to know that I am coming. I have the money for the plane ticket and am ready to leave the day after I graduate here in July. I want to be with you and our Sara. I know you are upset with me and I should have called and written more but I just need to know if you want me to come. I can't say I'm sorry enough but believe me when I tell you that I want to be with you." Alan poured out in a single breath.

Meg's insides took another leap. What was this new sensation?

Meg looked directly at The Mother as her anger and relief bubbled up and out from her and said, "Yes I want you to come. I don't want to make any promises and I don't want you to make any either but I want you to come."

The Mother froze in her tracks, her own anger finally unmasked. She made it perfectly clear with that one look that she was not happy about this development. She was going to pull out all of the stops on this one and there would be no safe harbor or mercy for the enemy.

"Good!" the relief in Alan's voice was palpable. Meg felt some-thing, but couldn't describe it.

"I will get my ticket for the day after graduation here. Will you pick me up at the airport?" he asked.

"What day is that? I might have to work but my mother will be happy to pick you up at the airport. I will see if I can get that day off for sure. It will be good to see you." Meg took in a sharp breath. Why did I say that? She thought. Had hope arrived? She realized now that that was what she was feeling and it scared the hell out of her.

"I can't wait to see you! Can I call again? When is a good time? A month seems too long to wait. I hope it goes by fast. I really have missed you, I hope you can believe that. I promise I will explain everything. I was so scared you wouldn't talk to me." The words rushed out of Alan so fast that it took Meg a little while to catch up.

Meg sat and listened to Alan talk. With every word she could feel hope blossoming in her stomach. The Mother was scrubbing the counters again. That was always a bad sign - the beginning of the all too familiar escalation from frustration to violence. Meg held the baby tighter. The father was home, so The Mother would not lash out tonight. She would save it though. Tomorrow would be a bad day. Tonight though, right now in this moment, Meg felt hope for the first time in a long time, and allowed herself to drink it in.

CHAPTER 16
MARRIED

M eg sat on the couch with the book on her lap. She had not be able to concentrate on it for some time, so she had given up. She was so lost in her thoughts that she didn't realize her husband had come up behind her until he kissed the back of her neck.

She smiled as he greeted her with, "Hello beautiful. I hope you were thinking of me just now."

"Actually I was. Do you know you still have the power to make my insides leap by just the sound of your voice? What is the secret to your power over me, sir?" she said as she kissed his nose. She marveled at the sight of him still. She truly and absolutely adored him.

"I don't know, maybe it's my kisses, or maybe it's my tallness or maybe it's just the power of our love together. Or maybe you are just weird!" he said grinning. "Insides leaping...what did you eat for lunch?" grinning bigger still.

"Well that's the last time I compliment your mad skills at making me all warm for your form!" she said grinning back and hitting his arm.

"Only warm? I must be losing my touch or I just need to try a little harder..." he said kissing her again.

"Getting warmer..." she said around his lips as they covered hers.

Later as they lay on the couch wrapped up in a blanket he looked down at her. Concern was prominent in his eyes.

"Uh oh....why so serious?" she asked and nibbled on his hand.

"When I came in today you didn't notice me for the longest time. It was like you were lost in thought. You haven't looked like that in a long time. Are the flashbacks returning?" he asked quietly.

"No. I was just remembering. There's no pain in the memories, and hasn't been for a long time. I promise. I was actually thinking of the day you called and then came back to me. I am still so grateful that I have you. God is so good and His plan was perfect even though we weren't! So much has happened in between the time before we knew Him and now. Do you realize that we have been walking with Him for more than 20 years and to me it still feels new in so many ways? I see the fruit of the years with Him in our kids and grandkids and am so thankful for the time we have had. I wouldn't trade it. To be free from anger and pain and to know joy and happiness is the greatest gift. To know peace and to have rest, priceless! To feel like every day is a gift, and not a burden. And to have it all with you is more than I could ever have hoped for. I still adore you, sir...but don't let it go to your head.... there are limits to my adoration....remember that! I love another greater than you." she giggled and threw his hand down.

He caressed her brow and brushed her hair with his hand. "Seriously though, was that all you were thinking? You looked so serious and a little pale. Are you sure you are ok?" he asked as he stared into her eyes trying to gauge her wellbeing.

She stared back into his eyes hoping to convey without words that being here with him was all she needed. His love had always healed her, she knew, but did he really know that truth? The years fell away as she stared into his eyes.

Their reunion had been strained at first, especially with interference from The Mother and The Brother, but they had managed to talk and work things out because there was love at the foundation. Meg would not have been able to describe what she felt for Alan as Love, because the feelings at the time were so foreign. She knew she felt something fierce and protective for her baby. She had the same feelings for Alan. She couldn't have named it though.

They married a week after he came back to her. It was a rocky time when it should have been a happy one. The Mother pushed the marriage. Meg thought it was because The Mother was betting that Meg would never do it. Meg had stated outright several times that she didn't intend to marry anyone, ever. She had been a front row witness to the toxic relationship of The Mother and father and didn't want any part of it, didn't really believe a truly happy marriage could exist...until the ultimatum from The Mother came. The Mother emphatically stated that they could not live in her house and not be married, so either they get married or Alan had to leave. So Alan asked Meg to marry him for now, and forever. She found herself struggling with the decision. She hadn't told him about everything yet, and wanted to be fair and let him know what kind of person he was asking to marry. She felt she couldn't truly share her future with him, unless she first shared her past, however difficult that may be.

She spent the night after he proposed telling him everything. From the penny tree, the years of The Brother's beatings, The Mother's abuse and cruelty and her own unconscionable behavior.

She told him about the rape last. She made him promise to listen to it all before she would give any answer to his proposal.

When she finally finished, she felt like a dirty rag. Surely he wouldn't want her now. He had to see that her father was right… she wasn't worth feeding, let alone marrying. It was unfathomable to her that out of all the girls in the world, she could possibly be the one anyone would want the most. As she told her stories, with each one she became more and more convinced that her decision not to ever marry was the right one. She was never going to be alright. She was always going to be a broken mess. Most nights she still woke up screaming or in a cold sweat, and her ugliness ran so deep inside that she could do nothing to keep it from seeping out and infecting him too. No, she couldn't do that to him.

When he finally spoke, he had tears in his eyes. He looked at her and reaffirmed his love for her and his desire to marry her right away. Meg was dumbfounded, and she argued with him about how marrying she would ruin his life. She sent him to his room and told him he was crazy and that she wasn't going to marry anyone ever, and that was final. She was so confused by the feeling of true love and acceptance that she didn't yet know how to truly welcome it into her heart.

The next morning The Mother told Meg that she was taking her to the courthouse to sign papers so that Meg and Alan could be married. Meg was livid. She told The Mother that she didn't want to marry him and that she was sending him away, but The Mother insisted and either out of habit or fear, Meg went. The whole ride to the courthouse Meg thought, *you can sign papers but you can't make me say I do.*

Meg felt betrayed. She knew the mother hated Meg's happiness so much, she would surely send Alan away at the earliest opportunity. She thought The Mother would be happy to do it. Now she wondered if the thought of her being miserable by making Alan miserable was a more apt punishment for The Mother to enjoy for years to come. The Mother always needed new fodder to feed on and this might just do it for a while.

The Mother had to sign papers because Meg was still only 17. The Mother chattered on with the clerk about her reasons for doing it. What was a mother to do...after all the baby was already here and they weren't going to be living together in her house and not be married...ever the moral martyr in her own mind, her own self-created moral superiority allowed her to constantly paint more ways for Meg to sin.

On the way home The Mother told Meg that she was to tell Alan that she changed her mind, and would be glad to marry him the following week. Meg sat in silence and stared out the window. She would do no such thing. If The Mother wanted it, Meg would resist.

When Meg arrived home, she entered the house intending to go straight to her room with her baby, but was instead caught off guard by the presence of her grandmother, whom Meg loved.

"I hear there is to be a wedding! I have come to take you shopping! Every bride needs a trousseau, and I hear there is not much time!" With that Meg was whisked out to the car. She looked behind her at Alan who was standing in the hallway with a look of happy hope on his face. That melted the last of her resolve. She could not fight his face, nor her grandmother's optimism. She would say "I do" but would not say "obey," she decided.

The wedding was small - just some close family. Her grandmother and grandfather were there, as well as her Aunt and Uncle and their children, The Mother and father and younger brother also.

Meg didn't have a fancy wedding dress - she wore a dress she already had from her closet. It was the only one she owned, actually. Meg was nervous, and wrestled within herself, feeling that this was a huge mistake. She could never make Alan happy - she didn't even know how to make herself happy, after all. You can't give what you don't have. She thought about leaving, but The Mother had the younger brother near the door. Did The Mother suspect or was it just coincidence? Either way, there was no escape.

There was no music, no formality. Down the aisle she walked in her school dress and black pumps. Her grandmother had bought her a silk flower bouquet, and a beaded tiara creation for her hair. Meg tottered shakily down the aisle. She hated being on display, uncomfortable and unfamiliar in the feeling of positive gazes directed her way.

She looked to her right as she walked, and saw the faces of her family. It struck her how much they were really strangers to her. She held on to that. They were strangers, they didn't know her, so it didn't matter, it didn't count..... Anger stepped back up and Meg stood straighter, defiant almost, and lifted her head up and looked straight ahead.

Meg almost stumbled and fell right there. Her heart stopped and she couldn't breathe. There in front of her was Alan. He was wearing dress pants, a button down shirt with the collar open and the biggest, most wondrous smile she had ever seen! If one could project love as a physical force with just a look, he had managed it perfectly. She was still moving to her amazement - or was it the world that was spinning - propelling her forward until she was there next to him.

She could feel the heat emanating from his body, smell his aftershave, see his face radiantly, honestly happy. He took her hands and looked into her eyes and told her she was beautiful and she could see that he meant it. It startled her to see in his face the way he truly saw hers. He truly meant every word and vow he made to her that day. Every profession of love and commitment that came from his lips was ironclad and unbreakable. The feeling was dazzling.

As she looked into his face and received every word and spoke hers in return, she found herself grow stronger as she realized that she truly deeply madly loved him with everything she was and could be. She was both terrified and confident at what she was doing and the rush of feelings it engendered; terrified of letting him down because she was broken and ugly but confident that he would keep his commitment, and in his love for her. She so wanted to be worthy of the look of unashamed adoration on his face!

Numbness had left the building for the moment and the feelings were frightening and overwhelming but she embraced them. What had this boy - no, this man - done to her? He had opened a door and a fountain flowed within her. She found herself holding tighter to his hand and leaning longer into his embrace and when he kissed her as his bride, the world stopped!

There was nothing in that moment except the feel of him holding her, the smell of him, and the warmth of his lips pressed hard onto hers. She heard nothing except the heartbeat in her own ears and the sound of their breath. She needed him like she needed air to breathe. She shook at the thought of that. All too soon fear, doubt and anxiety made themselves known. As their kiss finished she looked into his face and saw the same look of adoration, happiness and utter joy. She pushed back for the first time in her life at the all too familiar emotions threatening to take her back into the shadowland where numbness and anger were waiting. To her amazement as she pushed they retreated. She tested it again as they moved slightly forward once more. Again they retreated. Could it be possible that she might have some control over them, rather than their complete control over her? She didn't have long to ponder it at the moment.

Suddenly she was being moved down the aisle into the warm embrace of her grandmother and grandfather. The rest of the afternoon was a blur as they all went back to The Mother and father's house for cake.

Meg held her baby tightly, and her husband's hand even tighter. Here within the span of her hands was her family, her future and her hope. He would protect her, love her and make her whole, and she would do everything she could to make him happy. She finally believed it with all of her heart and she embraced it fully.

CHAPTER 17

ROCKY ROAD

Those beginning years were rough and rocky for the young family. They had to live with The Mother and father for a while until Alan could get a good income going, but Alan was hardworking and diligent. He could now see plainly how The Mother mistreated Meg. The Mother had taken off all masks of pretense once the wedding was over. She had begun torturing the young couple within days of the wedding by asking Alan about their time apart. She would imply that he must have been having a good time so much so that he couldn't write. She reminded him frequently of her burden of having to take care of his responsibility and that she had never asked him for anything in return. Alan would not reply when she would begin her diatribes of his shortcomings and reminders of her generosity and provision. His lack of response vexed The Mother. She was baiting him and Meg with urgent frequency now, and their lack of response caused her to sink to lower and lower levels trying to get a fight going.

Alan began working two jobs, so he was gone most of the time, leaving Meg alone with The Mother's vicious insults and jibes. Meg pictured her much like a spider. The Mother would try different tactics to draw her into the web so she could suck the life out of her. The stress was wearing on Meg. She no longer had school as a respite, and she had quit her job to spend more time with her Sara. She secretly believed that The Mother was pushing them so hard because she no longer had control over Meg or the baby and knew they would soon be beyond her clutches.

When Alan would come home from his second job late at night he would be exhausted. Meg would feel elated to see him and be with him only to be disappointed when he would fall asleep so quickly.

She would lay there and watch him sleep. The feelings of guilt for needing him and hurt at feeling rejected warred within her. Often in his sleep he would reach out to her and draw her into his embrace. "This is enough." She would tell herself as she felt safe and comforted in his arms. Even in his sleep and exhaustion, he was trying to take care of her.

It was a long battle for Meg to replace the feelings of self-hatred and inadequacy with ones of love and security. As the weeks went by The Mother's instigations became more pointed and provocative. She would work on Meg's self-esteem by telling her that something must be amiss in the marriage because Meg looked more anguished than glowing, unlike a new bride should. She would say things to de-feminize Meg. How her hair had always been mousy and needed to be kept short and how the way it was now was so unattractive because Meg's face was too round for longer hair. She commented on Meg's weight and wondered aloud about the northern girls he must been seeing while Meg was taking care of his baby with The Mother 's generous help of course...The Mother would never leave that part out.

Alan could sense the ever increasing tension radiating from Meg. Her desperation to leave was intensifying, especially now that she felt she had something worth leaving for. She wouldn't tell him what The Mother was saying to her. It was nothing new for her to be assaulted this way by The Mother. The thing that was different now was that she actually cared that The Mother's slights might be true. Did he think her unattractive? Did he have other girls while they were separated? Was she lacking in comparison? Did he still want her? She was so afraid of the answers because she felt for sure they would not be in her favor. Her insecurity came out in other ways. She began to criticize him and say awful things to him when they were alone. He would be hurt and bewildered and try harder to spend more time with her. Things would be slightly better when they spent more time together, but it was abundantly clear that they needed to get out. Meg became increasingly tense as she saw some of The Mother's traits emerging in herself. The awful things she would say and didn't mean. The incessant nagging. As much as she didn't want to be like The Mother, she found that, to her dismay, in moments she embodied some of her worst traits. She couldn't seem to stop once she got going, lacking the tools to stop her anger when it flooded out from her. Unfortunately many of these untapped flows were directed towards her husband.

Insecurity reigned during these sessions and she felt and looked like a lunatic. Alan, to his credit, took the frequent onslaughts from his wife and did his best to mend them. Meg would feel awful afterward. She knew she was being cruel and unfair and horrid. She would tell herself to try harder to be nicer, after all he was here! She couldn't seem to keep herself from re-directing all of The Mother's anger onto Alan. She had finally gained the tools to let the insults bounce off of her, but she lacked the ability to direct them in a more productive direction. Meg had some sense that The Mother needed her to be unhappy, to be at odds with her husband, to be unsuccessful at maintaining a family. She sensed that The Mother's ultimate intention was to prove to Meg that she was and always will be a worthless waste of space and that Meg needed The Mother to be the savior. The former was always not far from Meg's mind but the latter she refused to give into. She would be free of The Mother at some point even if it meant a life on the street. She was sure Alan wouldn't let it come to that, but she was most sure that she would get out, no matter what it took or who made it out with her.

CHAPTER 18
LEARNING TO LIVE

After two months of marriage and frequent skirmishes, the couple finally moved out of The Mother's house with their Sara.

The tiny apartment wasn't much more than a roach infested cracker box but it was theirs! They had no furniture except for a table and chairs, two trunks, and a bed. They had saved up enough money to buy a tiny black and white TV so that Meg could at least have that to break up her days.

What should have been a good thing sent Meg into a spiral of depression. All she wanted to do was sleep but the nightmares and flashbacks were keeping her up so that she would end up staying up for several days straight. Now that she had space to let her protective wall down, all the horrible things lurking on the other side seemed to need to pass through her to escape once and for all. Now that she didn't need to live in constant survival mode, she realized she had to process the horrors of her youth, and sometimes that felt even harder.

She would spend her days with Sara, a toddler now. She was quickly becoming mobile, and would climb onto the trunk pull herself along its edge, learning to walk. Meg delighted in her baby girl, but her increasing fatigue was becoming a real problem. Meg was experiencing severe mood swings as well. She didn't know what was happening to her.

When she started throwing up one morning, she realized she might know what was going on. It had surpassed night terrors and become physical illness, independent of any symptoms. When her husband came home she had him take her to the local drug store to buy a pregnancy test. It was positive. It was happy news! Meg was ecstatic too. Her first pregnancy had been filled with stress and uncertainty brought on from outside circumstances and people. This time they were a family, and they were going to enjoy it! It was the first normal thing she would do as an adult - as adult as a seventeen year old could be.

Meg threw herself into preparation. She had called and told her grandmother the news and her grandmother was elated for her. Not an hour later The Mother was at her door wanting to know why she had not been called first. The Mother began a lecture on the "facts" as she saw them. First, they could not afford another baby on what Alan makes. Second, they could not live here with another baby. Third, Meg was not equipped to handle two babies by herself and The Mother was going to have to make sure things got done. Fourth, Alan would have to find a better job or join the military because she wasn't going to support them.

Meg argued back. They were not asking her for anything. They intended to do like everyone else does and work and make payments and live as a family. She wasn't expecting The Mother and father to support them. Meg was upset the rest of the day. Her happy moment had become tainted by the toxic attitudes of The Mother's need to insert herself into every crack of happiness that fissured in Meg's dark life. Meg sat alone with her baby girl toddling around and cooing. She smiled down at her darling and wondered if The Mother might be right. Could she handle two babies by herself? Could they ever be like normal people and do things on their own without her support? It seemed the answer for these questions came a week later when Alan was laid off. A week after that, they were moving back in with The Mother and father. The Mother gloated openly. Meg withdrew. She hadn't been physically hit by The Mother in more than a year but her looks and her words were just as effective as any physical blow to make Meg compliant.

Alan looked for work diligently, and continued to work what had been his second job. He picked up extra hours. The silver lining was that Alan was now able to spend more time with Meg and Sara. As a result the couple grew closer and stood united as a team against the Mother's unhealthy strategies for tearing them apart. She still managed to get her licks in but it was less frequent and less damaging than before.

Until the Older Brother moved back in.

The Mother and Older Brother became a force to be reckoned with for Meg and her husband. The Older Brother would tag along on job hunts with her husband, and Meg would feel pangs of betrayal. She didn't want her husband spending any time with her abuser. Nevertheless they got along together pretty well. Meg couldn't decide if this was better than them fighting, or not. When Alan was at work though, the Older Brother would torture Meg with stories he said Alan told him in confidence about his time up north when they were separated. He never gave details, only hints and innuendos to increase the anxiety. It was even worse when the Older Brother explained how he was filling her new husband in on who she really was with stories of his own. Meg could only imagine what vile vicious poison The Brother poured out.

She waited every night for Alan to come home and say something to her about what The Brother may have said to him. Alan never mentioned anything and always treated her like he was ecstatic to see her and inquired as to how she was feeling. He told her he was concerned because she looked so tired and wanted to know what he could do. She would just smile and crawl in his lap or lay her head on his chest and say, "this is enough."

Her stress grew exponentially as time went on. Meg became ill frequently, and the doctor had to continuously monitor her blood pressure and proteins. The doctor asked frequently if Meg needed to speak to someone. Meg always made light of everything while there and never spoke of the stress. Here she was, having to keep secrets from the outside again.

In her fifth month of pregnancy she came home from a doctor's appointment to find her husband and the Older Brother in the kitchen talking with The Mother. Meg's emergency alert system automatically switched on. What was going on? She walked over to her husband and took his hand. He looked up at her and grinned and said, "I am thinking about joining the Air Force on the buddy system with your brother. I'd like to talk to you about it. Would you allow me to take you out on a real date to discuss?"

Meg froze. She looked up at him and just nodded her head. That was a lot of stuff to process in a minute. Air Force, date night, dinner....

"Good! I will go change. How are you? How's the little guy? What'd the doc say? He asked as he led her by the hand to their room.

Once inside, he closed the door and turned to her looking very serious. "I am going to get you out of here. I don't care if it is the Air Force or the Army or the Coast Guard. I promised that I would take care of you and this is the one way right now that I know how. Let me get changed and we can talk at the restaurant so they don't overhear. Know this...I love you so much and I am sorry that I haven't taken you far away from them - but I will." Her husband kissed her soundly and turned to change his clothes. Meg stood there stunned. What just happened here? Was he telling her that he saw what they were too? Was he really trying to protect her from them? Was he saying that he knew she needed protection from them, and that he could be the one to do it?

While he changed, she got the diaper bag ready and changed the baby and strapped a fresh sundress onto the wiggly toddler.

At the restaurant Alan explained everything that he had been seeing and hearing from The Mother and Brother. He was just sorry he hadn't made the decision to go into the military sooner so as to save her the stress. He apologized for not being able to make it on his own and having to put her back in that house.

Meg marveled at her husband....*he* was sorry? He had nothing to be sorry for. *She* had brought them into the spider's Lair - both her husband and child. They were trapped because she was trapped.

Her husband explained that he felt that The Mother would make it more difficult for both of them if he had just gone and signed up and headed out. So he talked the Older Brother into signing up too - that way The Mother would be less of a pain and it would get the Older Brother out to boot camp at the same time as Alan, leaving Meg some peace until they could move. He realized she would have to be alone for those weeks with The Mother, but if she felt like she could do it then he would sign up tomorrow and get the ball rolling.

Meg looked her husband in the eye and said firmly, "Do it. I can do it. Sign up let's go." And she leaned across the table and pulled him to her and kissed him hard on the mouth. "I love you." she said.

He grinned so big she thought his mouth would split. "That's the first time I have ever heard you say it like that. Like you mean it, like it's something....more."

Meg actually blushed! "I'm sure it's just the pregnancy hormones, I'll most likely be over it by tomorrow." she said grinning herself and rolling her eyes.

He took her hands in his and kissed them as he continued to smile and stare at her in that way that made her insides jump. When the food arrived she busied herself making a plate for their active toddler and herself. They relaxed and just enjoyed each other for the rest of the night.

CHAPTER 19

NEW BEGINNINGS

"Off we go baby girl!" Alan said as he held her hand in one of his and carried the car carrier with their 6 week old infant son in it. Meg held tight to her husband's hand and the hand of her 18 month old toddler.

She loved it when he called her baby girl. It made her feel safe and warm. She needed that now. She had spent the last several months in The Mother and father's house awaiting the arrival of their second child and the move to their new life.

Alan had ended up joining the Army instead of the Air Force which was all the same to her. They had been apart longer than planned due to her health. It had not been an easy pregnancy, requiring bed rest and frequent doctor visits and ending in the baby coming almost a month early. He was here now though, and he was fine and so was she.

The next few years were a blur - going from one base to another. They finally settled in Germany as their third post. They both loved it there. It was a harder post than the last one in Washington State. In Germany Alan was gone more frequently, anywhere from two weeks to two months. Meg had blossomed in the years away from The Mother. She was strong and unafraid. She frequently found new and interesting things to occupy her time....not that having two children and a husband didn't take up most of it! When she removed the fear from life, all that was left was joy and adventure. She was like a sponge - learning everything she could about the cultures she found herself in. She taught the children as well, always creating new projects and games for them.

The nightmares and flashbacks persisted; though she slept more than before, it was still not a completely restful sleep. She managed to keep it together for the most part, but had frequent outbursts of anger or frustration when the loneliness and responsibilities got to be too much sometimes. She could almost time them to the calendar. Alan began to understand the patterns as well. He couldn't do anything about his work schedule so he encouraged her in her projects and her excursions in the local community. She had made several friends who were Greek, German and Italian. She spent a lot of time with the kids at a local guesthouse run by the Greek family. It made it much easier while Alan was away, and a lot less lonely.

During one of Alan's extended absences, Meg was much more agitated. The Mother had been sending letters that were baited with painful reminders of Meg's unworthiness. She wrote of the Older Brother's exceptional service until he was forced to leave the military due to an injury. By this time the middle brother had been put out of the navy due to injury as well. The Mother wrote of her disappointment that she had not yet received pictures from Meg of her grandchildren, or the German countryside. The Mother so hoped that it was because the couple was busy with life, and not because things were amiss in their marriage. She would hate to have a repeat of their last move home.

Meg seethed over the letter, its' innuendos and reminders of her failure. She had crumpled it up and thrown it in the trash. Lost in her outrage Meg didn't see a toy car on the floor, and stepped on it squarely. Pain ripped through her foot and in reaction she grabbed the car and threw it across the room where it hit the wall with a resounding "smack!" and shattered into a million pieces of shrapnel. Sara, who had been playing on the floor across the room, became frightened and started to wail. All of the anger drained from Meg as she heard the cry of fear from her child. She ran quickly to the babe and picked her up to comfort her. Meg knew at that point that she could never lose control around her children, ever. She knew she had the potential to abuse just like The Mother. She could not be like that. She would not.

The next day Meg bundled up her precious ones and dropped them at an Army day care facility. She then walked straight to the Army Community Services, and asked for help. It was the first time in her life that she had ever said those words aloud. She had kept the family secrets because you did *not* share family secrets - ever. But years and years of bottling the pain and the hurt and the anger inside meant that now they were seeping out in a concoction of uncontrolled rage, like a festering infection. She would not pass on the pain or the dysfunction to her children if there was a way to avoid or mitigate it, to get the rot out from the inside before it could escape out of her.

Meg signed up for parenting classes and enrolled in other programs on budgeting and home maintenance. She eventually became a volunteer for their "Parents Encouraging Parents" program, and then finally employed as a family advocate. They trained her and sent her to school. It changed everything. She had never lost her dream of becoming a teacher and now in her own way, she really was one. She was teaching classes to parents on the importance of open communication and proper discipline and nutrition. She trained other volunteers as well.

She was advancing in her life toward something more, but at the same time the nightmares and flashbacks were her constant reminder that there was still something fundamentally broken inside her. The flashbacks of The Brother and Mother beating her were coming more frequently as she worked with child abuse cases in her job. She would feel physically ill as she read the reports. They were so similar to her own abuse - some worse, some not as bad, all wrong.

She had to leave work early one day after reading a report of a six-year-old girl who had allegedly been molested by her nine-year-old brother, and had welts from a whipping her mother gave her after the little girl told her what her brother had done to her. The Mother called the little a girl a liar and whipped her for lying. The neighbor heard the little girl screaming and called the MP's who found her in her bed crying, hysterically crying out, "I'm sorry mommy," over and over again.

Meg went to the daycare and bundled up her children hugged them hard and took them out for ice cream as a treat. Meg told her children frequently that she loved and adored them and that they were special and beautiful.

When her husband came home that night she had a special dinner made and a relaxing evening planned. The children were already bathed and in their jammies at the supper table. A movie was in the VCR waiting for them all to snuggle up on the couch and watch. It was a good night but it didn't keep the nightmare away.

She woke up in a sweat, crying and lashing out with her hands trying to figure out where she was. Her husband tried slowly and carefully to calm her down with his voice low and soothing. He knew better than to touch her when she was like this. He just kept a calm and steady cadence of "It's ok, you're ok, you're safe, I'm here. Just breathe through it, baby girl." Eventually she would realize where she was and fall into her husband's arms and allow him to comfort her. She would cry herself exhausted, eventually falling exhausted into a fitful sleep, and he would continue to rock her and hold her tight.

The next morning he pulled her to him in the kitchen and looked her in the eyes.

"That was a bad one. Do you want to talk about it? Actually let me put it this way...you need to talk about it. What happened yesterday?"

She put her head down and moved out of his arms, busying herself in the kitchen with breakfast. She was always embarrassed afterward - or was it ashamed? Either way she didn't like to feel so vulnerable, especially in the light of day.

"The usual. Nightmare followed by hysterics followed by uncontrolled crying and eventually sleep. How did you sleep? Coffee?"

"Come on hon. Don't shut me out of this. That was not 'the usual' by any standard. What brought this on? Something at work?" He was really worried this time.

"Well yeah it was something from work. Just a bad case with familiar circumstances. I'm sorry you have to live with and through my lunacy. I probably need to take a break from the office for a while. I can see if I can work at the commissary or something. I hate it that no matter how much I learn, I can't put these abused children back together again. All I can think about is what that little girl has ahead of her. At least she has a group of people looking out for her through family advocacy this time. Maybe she has a better shot at getting help early, so she won't be messed up like me."

"You're not messed up, sweetie." he said stroking her hair.

"Yes I am. It's the only thing I'm ever sure of." she stated matter-of-factly. Anger began to knock and she gave it limited permission. "What really gets me is that after all this time it still affects everything in my life. I have taken all of the classes on Anger Management and Communication Skills and Effective Parenting and Marriage and I have worked through so much of it and I get a job I love and now here I am failing once again and having to give it up because of something someone else did to me. And they - my family - could care less about me or how I am. And whenever I go home it's always the same. They brag openly about how they beat me and what a horrible person I am and how I won't amount to anything. They laugh at me like what they did was funny and like I deserved it. They will never apologize or even see that they were ever wrong. After all how could it be wrong to openly try to destroy something that you feel is beneath you and worthless? I say 'something' because you can't do what they did and see your victim as a human being. They were monsters then and they are monsters now. And it *still gets to me.*" At that she reigned in anger and took a deep breath, feeling guilty about the 'monsters' comment.

"Now I'm sorry but I am going to have quit my job today and I don't want you to be angry or worry about the money. I will go to the job store and see what might be open." She said as she pushed past him. "I'm sorry that I'm letting you down but I can't do it anymore."

"Stop...hon...wait. I'm not mad and I'm not worried about the money and you are not letting me down. I understand. Why don't you wait on the new job? Take a break, regroup, find a project or something or just spend time with the kids and me. Relax. We will work it out." He said, pulling her to his chest and petting her hair.

She let him hold her and she breathed deeply, inhaling all the lovely, familiar scents of him and her and their life together. She wrapped her arms around him and closed her eyes and let the tears fall and thought, "but if I don't do something how will I be worth feeding?" she shuddered and he pulled her tighter to him.

CHAPTER 20

LIFE

Five years had passed like a whirlwind. Meg, her husband, and the two children were now living in The South again having returned two years before from Germany.

Meg still struggled with nightmares and flashbacks. They never seemed to subside. She spent a huge amount of energy and time trying to keep them at bay so that she could function. She was exhausted all of the time, constantly under the pressure her emotions and memories put on her. She felt completely dead inside again. She couldn't sleep, thought that everyone would be better off without her. She had started drinking heavily at night, trying to drown out the flashbacks and find some form of the sleep that constantly eluded her. She lived from moment to moment, not registering the time passing and barely engaged in the everyday life of her family. She went through the motions of raising her children and housekeeping but was a shadow of a person again, alive and breathing but not really fully living.

A lot had happened in the last five years. She had registered some significant losses. Her beloved grandmother and her favorite aunt had died in rapid succession while Meg was overseas which drew heavily on Meg's mind. The little kindness she had known in her extended family, gone. She withdrew further and further away from her husband. Meg's only outward emotions seemed to be anger, depression and rage, usually taken out on her husband. She managed during the times he was gone with the children. Though she had never and would never abuse the children, the constant stress of nightmares and flashbacks were clearly taking their toll on her emotional stability. She could no longer avoid them nor could she control when they came, how long they lasted or how intense they were. She became afraid of the outside world, staying in the apartment unless she absolutely had to go out - and even then she would continuously scan the environment looking for threats. Meg feared that she was losing her mind and felt that she might be going crazy.

Alan was growing more and more concerned about Meg. Even though he understood and knew where the pain came from, it was still painful when she would unload a barrage of rage filled vicious words. Though he understood the source, they still had effects. Deep down he knew those words were meant for those who had truly hurt her, and not for him. He could see the prison constructed bar by bar from childhood, and knew that The Mother was the architect. He knew that Meg still felt jailed by walls built so many years ago, and that their imprisonment made her feel powerless and angry. Meg's rages usually followed some contact with The Mother. It was as if from afar The Mother could expertly plant the knife in his wife's gut and twist ever so slowly with her words inflicting as much damage as she could, with a surgical strike leaving his wife wounded and bloodied and in pain.

"The Mother is always to blame according to the children. Well they are finding out now that they are parents how hard it is! They are payin' for their raisin' like I had to! When they can't cope they blame me. I won't apologize for doing everything I could to give them everything or for speaking my mind when they don't like it or for cuffin' them when they needed it. I wouldn't change a thing, I'd do it again!!"

Alan had heard it all for years. He had always found it surreal that The Mother felt her behavior was exemplary and martyred. The Mother would tell Meg, "You know you were raised in a male chauvinist home!" as a way of deflecting blame from herself to the father or brothers.

The last several years had revealed just how deeply damaged Meg was from the consistent battery and verbal abuse at the hands of the Older Brother and the verbal and physical assaults of The Mother and middle brother. Meg had told him that she never felt safe anywhere because one of them was always waiting to pounce at something she did or didn't do. Meg would feel the tension and the build up to a blow up and sometimes would purposely provoke someone just to get it over with. She knew it was coming and they messed with her ahead of time and sometimes she just needed to take back some control so when she provoked it was some sick way of being in control of even just the timing of it. Meg had acted out in other ways as well. She consistently evaded and lied to The Mother and brothers. The Mother would never believe the truth when it was told and would scream and hit Meg until Meg said what The Mother wanted to hear which usually meant Meg had to admit to whatever evil The Mother believed she had done. Once Meg admitted to whatever The Mother accused her of Meg would be slapped around more, ridiculed and called vicious names and finally, (blessedly) sent to her room to "get out of my sight."

Meg learned that the truth was dangerous and it was best to stay away from it and say whatever The Mother wanted to hear even if it meant being called a "whore" or something equally as vile. It was less damaging than the telling the truth and enduring the unending wrath until you admitted to the lie she had dreamed up.

Alan saw his wife not as a victim, but as a survivor. He saw her strength and determination to not be like The Mother or The

Brothers. He saw her battle against the nightmares and the flash-backs. He saw how hard she fought to stay with them when she wanted to run. He could see the battle for self-esteem when she asked him how he could love someone as ugly as her. She didn't think it was possible that he or anyone could truly love her and didn't understand why he stayed. If her own parents couldn't love her because she was so awful (as she was reminded of frequently by The Mother) how could anyone love her? After all, her own father had told her she wasn't worth feeding. That's a pretty sad indict-ment against her being of value to anyone. But Alan did love her and he hurt when she hurt and he felt at a loss as to how to help her.

Alan didn't have the tools to fight for her so he endured, hop-ing and waiting for the day that she would see what he saw in her... a beautiful, tough, wonderful woman with strength and courage he wished he possessed. She had already been proven in strength, having survived so much. This he could not fathom. The fact that she felt responsible for other's mistreatment and abuse of her was painful for him to hear.

Meg remembered having gotten hung up on an electric fence at 3 years old and The Mother sent the Older Brother to pull her off. He was six years old. Every time he tried to touch her, he would be electrocuted as well and so he stopped trying after the second time. The Mother was screaming at him, and at Meg, and finally got a big tree branch and swung it around and knocked The Brother to the ground by accident, and then pushed Meg off. The Brother swore that The Mother was trying to kill him because he would not save Meg. Thus his hatred of her began that early, and The Mother perpetuated it and played on it. The Mother did not take either child to the hospital.

Meg remembered standing in the kitchen crying with her hand and thumb throbbing painfully while her mother was on the telephone with someone telling them how bad Meg had been to be down by the fence where she knew she wasn't allowed to be. Even at three Meg was supposed to know danger...not that The Mother was remiss for not watching her children properly....no it was Meg's fault. Meg had laid down on the floor and cried herself to sleep with no comfort from The Mother whatsoever.

Alan knew the story to be true as he had heard the Older Brother and Mother both tell it with Meg being at fault for not being where she was supposed to be. Alan was horrified at the story and their take on it. Meg never even thought that it wasn't her fault. She took the blame readily for anything they wanted to dish out to her and berated herself for days.

No, he would never leave her. He made it his life's mission to get Meg to see herself as he saw her, and to see her healed and secure and in his arms as a whole person. It was not an easy mission and would take some time to complete.

CHAPTER 21

PRAYER

"This can't be happening! Oh my God! Oh my God! I'm a widow!!" she screamed at the television. "Oh God, I'm a widow!!"

She fell to her knees on the floor as the news coverage continued to show the barracks on fire and more missiles striking around the burning structure. She could barely see as the tears flowed freely and the air in her lungs caught tight in her chest.

"Oh God...oh God....please....!" she mumbled weakly into her balled fists.

"Oh my God..." she thought. Is that how you pray? The guy she had been watching on TV for a few weeks now prayed but was she doing it right? She fought for control and thought back to when she had first started watching the evangelist on TV to remember at least one prayer he had said, or at least get a general formula.

Another two years had passed. Alan was still in the Army and they were stationed in North Carolina. He was being deployed to Saudi Arabia with his unit for Operation Desert Storm as part of the effort to expel Iraqi forces from Kuwait. Her husband would first be going to Riyadh for staging and then wherever they needed him. That was all Meg knew. She had moved with the children to her childhood hometown where she and her husband thought she would have support from Alan's family and her maternal grandmother.

Alan had helped them get settled, and then deployed 3 weeks ago. She had been watching the war live with every other American on CNN. She had last heard from her husband six days ago to say that he made it to his zone, it was hot, and that he would be out of communications for the foreseeable future but that he would write when he could. He told her how much he loved her and the kids, and that he would be home as soon as this was over. He told her he knew she could do this and that she was the strongest person he knew, to kiss the kids and that he hoped to be home by Easter. She told him she loved him too and that he needed to be careful and that she would be waiting. And then they said goodbye.

The Mother and Meg had started talking recently, after three years of no contact on Meg's part. She had had enough and during their last conversation said something awful and hung up, and hadn't taken a phone call from her since her husband had been getting ready to deploy.

She had now recently spoken with The Mother, and The Mother wanted Meg and the children to move in with them. Meg said no to that because she wanted to give it time to see the possibility of mending their relationship slowly. The Mother assured her that things were different that she was different. Meg didn't believe it but was willing, from a distance, to open a dialog. Her parents had moved back up North - they were now one state and three hours away now that the family had moved back home.

In the past ten days, Meg had felt overwhelmed and crippled by the absence of her husband. What was wrong with her? He had been gone before, why was she now responding so differently? It was different. This wasn't a field exercise or a simulation, it was the real deal, war. While he was still with her those last few days she could feel herself withdrawing from him, almost as if he had already died. Was it possible that she knew then?

Meg fought against the rising panic and began to think back over what she had learned.

She had listened to the tapes over and over again in the recent weeks. The Mother had asked her to make copies of them for the younger brother who was in Korea. She had started taping them because it gave her something to do and ended up listening to them at the same time. She had never had much contact with religious stuff. The middle brother had "gotten saved" a few years back and had called her frequently to tell her she was going to hell and that she needed to be led to Jesus by him. She told him that if she was going to hell then she would go on her own. She didn't need a crutch and she didn't need him telling her anything about God or hell or anything in between. He had been persistent until she asked him, "Why do I need this Jesus guy? Why? If it's just about not going to hell than your God could just grant me a pass. Why do I need the Jesus guy? If he doesn't want me to go hell or if he is going to send me to hell anyway why doesn't he just show himself?"

The brother had been silent. He didn't have an answer beyond "so you don't go to hell." Not very compelling of a threat, the hell thing, considering she didn't believe in hell or God or the devil or any of the other garbage he was spouting.

"That's what I thought." She said and hung up.

Now as she listened to the tapes she heard a different version of the Jesus guy. She was convinced that the middle brother didn't know this Jesus that the evangelist guy was talking about. The Brother had talked about him sending her to hell if she didn't believe and even if she did believe he may send her anyway. The evangelist guy talked about Jesus giving heaven as a free gift to those who believed because hell wasn't created for people, but was a consequence of sin. He talked about how before God created one blade of grass, that He knew who Meg was going to be, what she would do every step of the way, and that He allowed her to be born anyway in the hopes that they could meet and she might choose Him. The preacher talked about how much God wanted a relationship with her and wanted her to be His Meg and give her eternal life and make her a blessing.

Very compelling. He had hit all of the wish list items in her heart. To be wanted, to belong, to have a relationship and be cared for and to be useful, maybe worth feeding...very, very compelling.

She had hurried to make tapes for the younger brother and bootlegged a copy for herself. She didn't tell The Mother about her copy. She didn't want anyone to know she was even thinking about getting religious. Besides, she needed to hear more before she fell for anything that The Mother or middle brother were involved in. They couldn't be trusted, so anything they dangled in front of her was suspect from jump.

Meg listened to the tapes at night when she was sure no one would come by or bother her on the phone. She would draw the curtains and turn out most of the lights except for a small lamp and take notes as the evangelist spoke about God and the Jesus guy.

She was starting to want what the man was talking about. She wanted to live a life of abundance where she was loved and accepted, wanted even. She felt guilty for even believing it was possible for God to love her after everything she had done. How could it be that the God of the universe even knew she existed let alone everything about her like the man said? He kept talking about how God cared for His creation and that the life she had lived apart from Him was not the one He intended for her. She listened as he talked about God giving man "free will" to choose Him or not and that it made a difference. If you didn't live with Him in your life you didn't have access to everything He made for you. Kind of like paying for an all access pass to your favorite music group, only Jesus was the one who paid your entry fee. She listened to how much God loved us and the fact that Jesus decided to go to the cross before she was even born paying the penalty for her crap. He explained that it wasn't like the genie in the bottle thing where you rubbed the lamp and got your three wishes granted. He would give you a new life if you allowed Him to lead you on the path and be in a relationship.

Was it possible? Could it be true? Was this Jesus guy the evangelist was talking about really legit, or was it another story like Santa Claus?

She listened to the tapes three times over, which took up the majority of three weeks' time. She got to the point where she needed to know more. The evangelist kept referring to the Scriptures or the Bible, but she didn't know at the time that they were the same thing. She didn't own a Bible, so she thought she might go and get one, and see if what the guy said was true.

After going to several, she realized that she couldn't buy a Bible in a grocery store. She ended up driving twenty miles out of town to a book store and bought the smallest, most compact Bible she could find, and made them put it in a brown paper bag so no one would know what it was. She was tough and she didn't want anyone to think she had a weakness, so she took it home and hid it in the couch. She had never had a problem walking a bottle of Bacardi or Southern Comfort right down the street for all to see, but a Bible was a big problem for her! She would pull it out at night and read it by the small pool of light cast by her lamp, as she listened to the evangelist talk.

Finally she realized a couple of things. First, this Jesus guy was for real and she believed everything this evangelist said about Him because she could find it in the Bible just like he said. Second, she realized her condition; that apart from a relationship with Jesus and God she would never reach the true potential and purpose for which he had created her, and that her sin unrepented would keep her separated from Him. Third, she realized that through His eyes she had value and was worth His own life being poured out. That was the hardest to accept. Her earthly father had not shown her love like that - or love at all, really - so it was hard to believe that a heavenly father would sacrifice himself for her just so she could know Him and walk with him.

He thought she was not only worth feeding, but worth dying for. Lastly, she knew that she wanted it with everything in her being. She wanted to belong to the Father and to be part of His kingdom and His ways. She sought the peace and comfort of His words and the security that could be found in faith in Him.

But she was hesitant. She still had so many unanswered questions. As she sat there that night, she turned on the TV channel surfing trying to quiet her thoughts. As she pushed the remote from channel to channel she only paused briefly at each one before moving on. She really wasn't looking for anything, she was just doing it by rote until she heard a familiar voice.

Meg froze as she listened. Could it be? It was! It was the evangelist from the tapes! And he was on in the middle of the night so no one would know she was watching him! What a happy coincidence!

She listened to him night after night. Another happy coincidence, the man was on every night and even was on Sunday mornings. She listened like a starving man who had just found an abundance of food. She would get the Bible out of its hiding place and read along with him. She found strength and peace in what she was seeing and hearing. The hunger for her to be a part of God's family grew but still she hesitated. Every night the man would give an opportunity to receive Jesus and she would turn it off before the prayer.

This night as she stood in her living room watching the SCUD missiles impact the buildings on CNN and she was crying out "Oh my God I'm a widow!" she paused in her panic and thought, "Oh my...God...is that how you pray? Well God if you are there as the man says, then I need to know that my husband is ok." She continued to watch the news reports almost every minute for 2 days. She was fixing the kids dinner when the phone rang. As she made her way across the room to answer it, her eyes never left the TV.

"Hello?" she said distracted.

"I'm OK, hon...can you hear me? I'm OK."

Meg's breath caught in her throat. Was she dreaming or was that her husband's voice? She took a ragged breath and his name came out in a whisper.

"Yes hon, it's me. I'm OK. I just now got a chance to call and I don't have long but I want you to know that I love you so much and I miss you and I'm ok."

She said his name again and as she heard her own voice she realized that she was crying. Tears were streaming down her face. "I was afraid that you were dead! I was waiting for someone to come to tell me you were dead! I love you too! Listen, you have to come home to me! I can't do this without you!" She realized she was babbling but it all just poured out.

"I will baby girl, I promise! Nothing can keep me from coming home to you and the kids. How are they? How are you? I know how hard it must be and I really wish I was there to hug you all and I'm sorry you were scared. I should be able to call more and at least write more now that we are stationary. Look, I'm out of time and I have to go but I'm going to try and call in the next day or two. Don't be afraid, baby doll. I will be home as soon as I can. I love you so much."

"I love you too so much. Please be careful! We are ok don't worry about us just take care of yourself! Please come home to me. I miss you so much! It's so good to hear your voice!" She was still crying and didn't know how to stop. She realized that this was the first time she had cried in years, the first time she *felt* anything. What was happening to her?

"I gotta go hon. I love you and I will call as soon as I can. I don't want to go. I wish I had more time. Love you. Bye."

"Love you too, bye." and then he was gone.

She could smell the chicken nuggets starting to burn. She put the phone down and hurried to the kitchen glad to have something pressing to do. She finished getting dinner ready and called the kids to the table.

"Mom, were you crying?" Sara asked concerned.

"Um...yeah I guess I was. That was daddy on the phone. He said he is ok and that he loves and misses you both so much! He wants you to know that he is going to be home as soon as he can."

"Can I talk to him?" Her son asked, excited.

Meg immediately felt bad...she hadn't even thought to call them to the phone. She had been in such a state of shock at hearing his voice.

"He said he would be calling back in a day or two and I promise you can talk to him then. I'm sorry bud, but he only had a minute. He wanted to talk to you and your sister too."

They finished dinner, talking about what the first things they wanted to do when daddy came home. They cleaned up the dinner dishes and the kids got their baths and snuggled down on the couch with their mother. This was flat out her favorite time of day. Her Sara was seven now, and her son, Adam, would be turning six in a few months. She had loved every age they had been, and tried to give them at least some semblance of security and maternal care.

As they sat together, she read from the Arabian Nights. This was something she had done since their infancy. She still read them bedtime stories. They still seemed to love it. She would embellish them with silly voices and dramatic pauses and much fanfare. They would get so into the story that the characters and landscapes would weave themselves into their dreams, which they would recount to her with rapture the next day. She would listen avidly, fascinated by their grasp of higher thoughts and complex imaginations.

That night after she put the kids to bed she took up her position on the couch and turned on the TV. She had a few hours until the evangelist would be on and she wanted to catch up with the news coverage. She only watched for about a half hour before the restlessness hit her.

What was happening to her? She *never* cried. Not for years. She couldn't remember the last time. It might have been the night her son was born when she learned that he was perfect - skinny - but perfect for coming almost a month early. "Yeah," she thought, "that was the last time."

She felt like crying now as she thought about her husband and what he had said to her. She allowed herself to finally feel - and the dam burst.

She sat on the couch alone, illuminated by the light of the TV, and cried until she was exhausted. At some point she must have fallen asleep. She woke to a pain in her neck only to realize that she was laying all bunched up on the edge of the couch and had somehow worked the Bible out of its accustomed spot stuffed between the cushion and the side and it had lodged itself in the crook of her neck. She dislodged it and slowly lifted her head up. She looked at the clock on the TV and realized it was time for the evangelist. She quickly turned to the right channel and found that he had already started. He was talking about how God knows what we have need of before we even ask and makes arrangements according to His purposes to fulfill our needs, even if it isn't exactly what we are asking for. What a coincidence! He was answering her questions.

She listened all the way to the end and as usual she turned off the TV right before he prayed. She put down the remote and sat on the edge of the couch fidgeting and then stood up in the middle of the room.

"Look. I believe everything that man has said about you. I believe that book over there. I believe you came down here and let yourself be born in this body and that you were perfect in it and that your mom was a virgin and that you died on that cross and rose from the dead. I can even believe that you did for me. I believe that your death was more than enough, like he said, to pay my debt for all the crap I've pulled and I want you to know that I'm sorry for all of it and that I want to pray that prayer and be yours but you gotta know...I gotta know.....look, I'm not trustworthy. I have never finished a single thing I have ever started. I am damaged from what has been done to me and what I have done to myself. I believe you can do what that man says and give me a new life and help me be a better person, mom and wife.

I gotta know that you are gonna hold onto me because I can walk away in a heartbeat, I've done it before. If I do this thing, I gotta know you won't let me go even when I hurt you and do dumb or destructive things to others or myself. I just gotta know. I don't ever want to start and not finish this race. If you don't want to take the bet on me then let's just part ways now. What do you say?"

With that she headed to her bed to see if she might be able to sleep or even have one of those dreams like the guy in the Old Testament who had ticked off his brothers to the point that they had finally sold him. It had turned out good in the end for him, but man he had walked a rocky road to get there!

CHAPTER 22

SALVATION

Meg had slept but she didn't feel truly refreshed. She got the kids off to school and laid down on the couch again, kicking herself because she had forgotten to put the Bible away in its hiding place. Good thing no one had noticed it.

As she lay on the couch, she pondered her sleep. She didn't dream per se, it was more of a cascade of images, none of them taking hold or fully forming. Kind of like birds flying overhead but none of them landed or got close enough to identify. It was strange; she had never experienced that sensation before.

At some point she fell asleep and awoke to the phone ringing. She quickly jumped up to answer it.

"Hello?" she said. Wow, I sound groggy, like I just woke up, she thought.

"Hey baby girl! How's my baby doing? I miss you and I couldn't wait until tonight so I ran here instead of the chow hall. I'm not missing much for dinner I think." her husband said snickering.

"I'm fine! It's so good to hear your voice! The kids miss you as much as I do. I felt so bad that I didn't call them to the phone last night. They are at school now, will you be able to call back when they are home or is this it for now? Are you good, I mean taking care of yourself? I wish you were here - I sleep a lot better when you are here to help when the bad dreams come."

"Are they bad, are they hurting you too much? I wish I could hold you right now and make you feel better. I'm sorry I'm not there. Please believe me when I say that I love you so much and will do anything to get home as soon as I can. Can you hold on a little while longer? Hey, do you feel that?"

"Feel what?" she asked startled.

"Me hugging you. I have my arms around you right now. I'm never letting go of you baby girl."

Meg smiled at that and felt a warm flush creeping into her cheeks and neck. What was happening to her? Where was all this mushy, gooey, feely stuff coming from and worse yet what did she do with it?

"I'm holding you too and I'm never letting go either, um bub-bykins." She felt awkward using the silly endearment but he was so natural at them.

He laughed out loud. "Bubbykins!!! I'll take it! Where did you come up with that, I love it!"

"I dunno. It just came out there. I'll just call you 'Kins for short. Don't make a big deal out of it." She said blushing again.

"They are calling me back. I will try and call tonight when the kids are home. I love you baby doll. Please take care and try to sleep. Remember I'm holding you and I'm not letting go, ever. After all, I'm your Bubbykins now." He said chuckling.

"Please be careful, Kins. I love you too and am holding you too. Get something to eat so I don't have to worry about that as well. Call tonight for the kids if you can. It will help them if they can talk to you. We are lonely without you. Talk to you tonight. Go eat, I mean it!"

"I will promise to go eat if you call me Kins again!" he said and she could hear the smile in his voice.

"Ok...Kins. Go eat! I love you." She said with a smile. This actually felt good....being a little gooey with him. She had never been comfortable showing affection verbally or otherwise. She was always waiting for some form of rebuff or rejection or ridicule. He never once gave her any reason not to trust him but she trusted no one. She could feel the walls she had put up around her shift a little, like tectonic plates years before an earthquake. They didn't fall, but they moved.

Her husband called back later that night and was able to talk for a little longer. He got on the phone with the kids and they filled him in on life without him. It shocked and surprised her to hear her Sara tell him that "Mom hasn't had too many nightmares, but she's had a few." She was mortified. She had no clue her Sara knew about the nightmares. She would have to work harder so her little ones wouldn't have to know anymore.

"Mom, dad says you have a new nickname for him and he wants to hear you call him that. What is it?" her son asked with his eyes all squinty, smiling.

"Never you mind. Is that my cue that he wants to talk to me again?" she said playfully patting him on the butt. "Move over little man so I can sit."

Her son said goodbye to his father and ran to his room to play before bath time.

"Outing me already are ya! Well, how shall I punish you for it!" she said smiling.

"I guess you will have to think of new and creative ways since we have some distance, but for now I want you to know I love you and I thank you for doing such a great job with the kids. I know it can't be easy. I miss them so much too. It's hard for me and I know it's hard for you and them too. I don't have much more time. I mailed a package today. I picked up a few things for you and the kids. I hope you like it. I will call again as soon as I can. Take care baby doll. I love you."

"Back at ya, Kins. I love you and you take care too. I'm still holding you." She said secretly pleased with herself that she was getting better at this.

"I love that, Don't stop! Gotta run. Bye my love."

"Bye."

She hung up the phone and wrapped her arms around herself and closed her eyes. She was holding him now. She was sending him all of her love. She could feel it and she liked it.

She hurried and put the kids to bed after reading their next Arabian Nights story and rushed to the TV to catch up on the war news and wait to hear what the evangelist was going to talk about tonight.

She remembered her speech in the middle of the room last night. She wondered how she would feel if Jesus decided she really wasn't a good bet. She knew what she would feel devastated, but she would also understand.

Finally the evangelist was on. His message tonight hit every concern she had about not being trustworthy or worthy at all. He talked about how Jesus was the friend that sticks closer than a brother and that he would never leave you or forsake you and that even if you walked away from him he would pursue you. Meg gave in at that point. It was almost as if God had heard her in the living room, and answered her through the evangelist. When the evangelist made the invitation that night to receive Christ she got down on her knees in front of the TV and closed her eyes and prayed the prayer for salvation and repentance. When it was over she turned off the TV and sat still on her knees. She didn't know what she should expect. He had said that all of heaven rejoices when one sinner comes to repentance in Christ. She wondered if she should be hearing "Hallelujah's" or angels singing. There was only silence, but still she sensed that something had changed. It was like a soft brush against her cheek, an acceptance, a caress, a quiet thing, an intimate thing.

She waited quietly for a few more minutes and then turned off the lights. She went to bed and slept the whole night through without a single nightmare or restless dream. For the first time in her life that she could remember, she woke up rested and refreshed. Her new life had begun and she was ecstatic.

CHAPTER 23

NEW LIFE

The weeks were flying by! Meg had hit the ground running with her newfound life. She voraciously devoured the Word of God (which she no longer hid in the couch). She spent every moment she could reading and studying and listening to the evangelist. It was like Dorothy from the Wizard of Oz opening the door and seeing her world go from gray to color. She felt awake for the first time.

One of the first things she did as a new Christian was to sit her two children down and talk to them about Jesus. Both of her children accepted Him according to the purity of their understanding as children.

She learned quickly however that coming to Christ didn't mean that everything in her life was fixed or rosy. She still had the troublesome memories and some flashbacks but she dealt with them differently. When they would come she would sit down and let them wash over her as she prayed for help. She found that it actually helped and felt that her prayers were heard as the intensity of the flashbacks lessened a little at a time. She was grateful for any relief at all from them. She was grateful period.

Her sleep had improved she was now getting three to four hours of sleep a night and the nightmares receded into the shadows. She felt less exhausted and more refreshed when she awoke.

She would talk to Alan at least once a week but she hadn't told him about her newfound salvation or her experience with the Jesus guy. It was too complicated to explain in five minutes over the phone and she didn't know what he would think about it all. She wanted to talk to him face to face. She wasn't sure how he would react. Being apart often felt like time was standing still - that they were just filling each other in in fits and starts, and that their growth together had been put on hold until his return. But she had grown so much - perhaps more than her whole life pulled together - in his absence! How could she explain that, and would he join her? Understand her?

He had been raised in church but had rarely talked about it the whole time they had known each other and had never talked about it being of any value. She wondered about that. How could he not have told her about the Jesus guy? The middle brother had continuously harassed her about getting saved and threatened her with hell and when she would talk to her husband about what The Brother had said she would be angry. Maybe that was it, he didn't want to risk her being angry at him for his belief? If he had a different view of the Jesus guy than her brother, wouldn't he have told her? She began to stew on it and actually became a little angry with her husband for not telling her anything. She would wait and have the conversation when they were together and find out what his thoughts and beliefs truly were.

Alan knew that something was different because when he talked to her on the phone she seemed happier - like light was seeping out from her in the same way that the darkness used to. He felt like she was in the moment with him and he had her full attention. For them, that was something of a miracle. She was no longer preoccupied inside her own head. There was an absence of intrusive thoughts which had previously been a constant. Before, it had been a fight for clarity to reign supreme over the constant crowding of chaos and pain battling and rattling around inside her head. Her mother's voice was an endless loop of malicious and maligning speech, like a stuck record with a scratching needle in her mind. She had seen a war movie once where a POW was placed in a room with loud music and voices shouting and flashes of images on a screen and frequent beatings for hours day after day. It was called re-education. That was what it had been like for her in The Mother's house, and Meg had never had a sense of safety or security or peace. It had been better since she and her husband had left and there was less contact with anyone in her family, but the images and words and beatings still played frequently in her head, and her mind made her body tense and respond as if it were still suffering the trauma directly.

Although now, everything had shifted a little bit. She found she could think more clearly. She could block out a lot of noise when she prayed and asked for help and as she learned more about Jesus. She was growing spiritually and it was effecting everything else in her life positively as well.

That March she got the phone call she had been waiting for. Her husband was coming home! It had been 4 months since she had seen him. She was so excited she was positively gushing as she talked to him about how much she couldn't wait to see him and how much she loved him and her feelings for him.

He was frankly mystified! She had never given so much emotion or talked about her feelings for him. She had always been cautious, mistrustful and closed. He knew she loved him but she had always been so guarded with herself because she didn't trust anyone not to hurt her. She hardly ever showed affection first. He would always initiate by holding her hand or brushing her hair or hugging her. She rarely initiated any of those things on her own.

She never made bids for his affection either; so he was at a loss for the origin of all of the changes he was sensing. He was glad to hear the words, but even happier to hear the affection behind them. He thought that maybe the extended time away from each must have made her want to open up to him more. He couldn't wait to see her and his children.

Meg and the children made their way back to the base in the south where she waited impatiently at the airfield for Alan's plane to land. She, Sara and Adam stood on the sideline with little American flags beating softly in a wind of anticipation and excitement. Sara and Adam were so excited to see Daddy come home. Adam was even more excited about the "airpane" daddy was on.

He is so adorable! Sara's hair is longer now and she is so big now! Meg thought looking at her babies.

She had bought a pretty new outfit and was hoping he would notice that she had lost a little weight…she blushed at the thought. She had never really been concerned with her appearance to this point because it was low on the priority list, way under survival from minute to minute. Now that the fog had lifted and she could see more clearly, she started to take notice of those things and move proactively to do something even though she felt woefully ill-equipped in the feminine department. All of this led to the image of her mother standing in front her laughing at her and telling her she "looked like a clown!" and to "get that stuff off her face!" when she had tried to experiment with the makeup a friend had given her. That wasn't enough though; The Mother had ridiculed her at the supper table with all The Brothers and the father present, piling on joke after joke, ridicule after ridicule. "Dogs don't wear makeup anyway do they?" "Hah like there's enough makeup in the world to cover that ugly mug!" "Like anyone would look at you anyway, dog." "Get back in your hole troll!"

As she stood there on the field awaiting her husband's arrival remembering the event, she began to shake, and wanted nothing more than to run and hide. What was she thinking trying to look pretty! She reached down and held her children's hands mostly to keep her in the here and now and to remind herself that she couldn't run. Their little hands, naive to the storm raging in her head, tethered her to the world. Then there was another thought... "Be still...I'm here and he is coming." It startled Meg...was she hearing things now...hallucinating....oh God was she going crazy? She heard it again in her head, "Be still...he's here." Instead of being afraid, she felt an instant calm wash over her body. She looked into the crowd of soldiers departing the plane she hadn't even seen arrive because she had been lost in the past.

They all looked the same to her, and she wasn't immediately able to distinguish Alan from the crowd. It wasn't until he was almost directly in front of her and saying "there's my baby girl!" that she began to run toward him.

Meg and the children leapt on him, and it was all he could do to remain standing. They were all crying and laughing and freakishly normal in their reactions. She kissed him repeatedly and took inventory to see that he was all there and that he truly was unharmed. The children clung to him as he picked them both up and hugged and kissed them and told them how big they had gotten and that they had a lot to do to catch up. He asked them about what night they were on in the Arabian Nights book, and that they were going to have to catch him up on all the ones he missed while he was away. The kids talked non-stop, trying to fill him in on four months' worth of school assignments and books and television and birthday parties and scraped knees.

Meg just stood there watching and thought about how this must be the way it was really supposed to be. It was surreal for her. Is this what normal looked like? She looked around at the other families in reunion and saw the same scenes and all of the sudden she felt something enormous.....she felt *connected*.

CHAPTER 24

REUNION

Alan's first few days home were a whirlwind, getting reacquainted with his little family. He gawked in amazement at his wife, who seemed to be a totally different person. She was more "there" somehow, and even bubbly sometimes! He didn't know what to make of it. He did notice that she was avoiding eye contact...a lot. It made him nervous. He felt as if there were something wonderful and awful going on and every time he would try to engage her in conversation about it she seemed to move out of his reach. Finally on the third night home he confronted her.

"What's wrong? You won't look at me. What did I do? Tell me what you are thinking, I don't know what's going on! Did something happen...did you have an affair, did someone hurt you? I can't stand it! What aren't you telling me?" His brave face was the mask of a tortured soul. She looked at him, startled by the amount of pain in his face. She hadn't realized ever before that her behavior or lack of affection had actually been painful for him. She took only a few seconds to berate herself. This was the awful part of being awake and aware she was really seeing how her stuff affected her husband and children, and it wasn't easy to know the extent of the damage she had done. It was still better than living in a constant haze of numbness though, she reminded herself.

She stepped away from him and put her head down and said, "Why didn't you tell me? You knew all this time, why didn't you tell me?" and she burst into tears...she couldn't believe it...she was actually crying!

Her crying startled him so much that he was frightened. She never cried. He went to her and tried to pull her to him and she moved back.

"I don't understand. Tell you what? What did I know? You are scaring me....tell you what?" He pleaded, confused.

She took a deep ragged breath and tried to talk but the words wouldn't come. She knew she was being ridiculous but she couldn't stop crying now that she had started and she didn't have much experience getting her emotions under control because she hadn't really had to before...she had always felt dead inside, flat, nothing except for anger.

This feeling was different, and she didn't even know its name. Her husband put his hand out and took hers and she let him. He moved a little closer and said, "Whatever this is we can work it out baby girl. No matter what it is, just tell me what it is." He was looking at her with such intensity as if willing her to speak the words. She kept taking short glances at his face but was unable to speak for another few minutes.

"Why didn't you tell me about Him? You were raised in church. You knew about Him and you never told me. Is it because you didn't think I was worth saving?" she sounded like a scared little girl and she supposed she was. She was terrified that he would answer yes to her last question just like her father had said she wasn't worth feeding...did he believe she wasn't worthy either? If he answered yes then she was sure she would be right back down the rabbit hole of despair because that would mean there was truly no hope for her.

He was taking too long to answer she thought. She stole a glance at his face and saw confusion, anxiety and other emotions she couldn't name. She looked at him more fully and he looked back at her, his eyes full of trepidation.

She pulled away and tried to take her hand back, taking his silence as an affirmation that he didn't believe her worthy of His love. She could feel herself starting to slip back inside herself, berating herself for even thinking that she could be different or that anyone could truly want her because she was not worth anything.

He stopped her from pulling away and looked at her and took her chin in his hand. "I'm trying to figure out what you mean but I want you to look at me. I have never and will never feel that you aren't worthy of anything. You deserve so much more than I can ever give you. I can't believe after all this time that you would think I find you unworthy of anything or that I would keep any good thing from you. Please believe me. What "Him" are you talking about? You asked why I didn't tell you about Him and about church...do you mean God?"

She looked at him with tears flowing and just nodded because again words were not possible in light of what she knew was the truth. He said he would never think her unworthy, as mind boggling as that was for her to believe. She wanted so badly to own that understanding, to live in it to be in acceptance of it, to be secure in it.

"Well yeah I went to church with my family but I was a kid and thought it was boring. It was just something we did. I can tell you some of the stories I remember but I don't know that I remember much else."

She stared at him. Could it be he hadn't told her because he didn't really know? She was dumbfounded. But how could he not know? He had been raised in a church, gone to Sunday school, got confirmed and baptized and all of that stuff? She had the certificates in a shoebox in the closet!!!!

She stopped crying and looked at him. "The Jesus guy...you know God's son, he came down was born of a virgin, lived a sinless life and died on the cross to save us from our sin and rose from the dead and wants to have a relationship with us now and give us eternal life and help live every day with Him while we are here." She explained that we weren't just random acts of biology like she had thought before but that God had created us each uniquely and specifically for a purpose and there was an actual (can you believe it!) plan for each one of us. That He loved us so much that he agreed to go to the cross before he ever created this planet. That he had allowed her to be born anyway knowing everything that she would do and all the mistakes and bad decisions she would make. That he had sent the Holy Spirit so that we can have access to the new life in Him and all the power and potential and help we need in our daily walk and that he would never leave them alone. The one who leads us and guides into truth and convicts the world of sin so that we know that we need the Jesus guy and he comes when we pray to make us born again.....all that stuff...." She trailed off because of the blank look on his face.

He didn't know. He doesn't know! She thought.

"I don't know what you are talking about. I have never heard this before. I just remember some stories and doing some singing and having to stand up and sit down a lot and having to say some creed thing. I guess it wasn't really registering." He said.

"Well then you need to get saved right now because I'm not going to do this without you!!!" With that she sat down and explained what had happened, how it happened and how things had changed and how much she was learning and how much she could finally sleep and on and on for what seemed like hours. She explained the message of salvation and asked him if he thought he wanted to do that and said it was ok if he needed time to process it all because she had.

He looked at her and said that he wanted to do it. The change he had seen in her and the words she had spoken and the message of salvation as she explained it to him had him convinced. She led him through the same prayer she had prayed and for the first time they were truly attached, totally one, and on their way to becoming a new whole, together.

Over the next few weeks they packed up and moved back to the base down south. The move went pretty smoothly as they both worked together with limited stress. She found that she enjoyed his company and was learning all kinds of new things about him as they talked and packed. She was dazzled by him anew. She found a deepening passion and love for him that she never thought was possible or even available to her. That she felt anything was a miracle but to experience this was way beyond anything she could even think to ask for.

CHAPTER 25
BOXES

Over the next two years Meg and her husband continued to grow together and spiritually. They would learn and study together when they could, but mostly it was her sprinting ahead as she was a stay at home mom and had the time.

Her nightmares began to be replaced by vivid and realistic dreams. She would dream of Jesus and over those two years He personally took her through a healing process where she began to recover from the worst of the pain.

The first night she dreamed of Him she was exhilarated and afraid. She was standing in what looked to be a warehouse full of boxes of different shapes and sizes. Some were small and they graduated up into the size and shape of a house. As she walked among them she began to feel tense and uneasy. There was something about them...something ominous and menacing and familiar. As she walked around the corner of one stack she saw Him standing there and smiling at her like he had been waiting for her and even - could it be possible? - like He was happy to see her!

Meg froze, unsure what to do. She stared at Him and He smiled invitingly back and began to walk toward her. He was dressed in white and seemed illuminated from within! He came to her and laughed as He picked her up in a bear hug. Meg actually giggled as he swung her in a circle. He kissed her on the cheek and said, "Meg, it's good to see you."

She sucked in a deep breath and held it. Was this real, or a dream? It felt real. She could even smell him and feel the texture of his clothes. He took ahold of her hands and she could feel the roughness of his palms against hers. She looked closer at his hands. She could the scars, a large elongated one on the back of his hand just above his wrist. She turned his hands over and saw the scars in between his palm and wrist. They were horrible looking - an almost transparent slip of skin over the wound that was hard to describe because she had never seen anything like it. His scars reminded her of the pain he must have suffered for her. She looked him in the face and could see the horrible scars there as well. They patterned his face and his chin and neck in a lattice-work of scar tissue that extended up to his brow line and receded back into his hair. She had only read about his injuries in the book and had heard the evangelist describe the horror of his abuse. She hadn't known what to expect, but it had not been this.

She wondered about the piercings in his side and looked down at his feet and again witnessed the horrible scars running between his feet and ankles. These were more horrific than his hands. They were jagged and elongated and looked truly horrible. She felt so unworthy. She had been beaten and penetrated and rejected but on some level she had always believed she deserved it or did something to cause it. He had done nothing to deserve it or cause it. He was an innocent. She stood there staring and warring inside herself.

He was shaking her hands now. "Meg, look at me." He said.

She looked up at him with tears in her eyes and looked directly into his. The love she saw there was unmistakable and overwhelming. If she could have built a home and lived in that look of true, pure love and belonging she would have paid any price!

"I have something for you. If you want it." He said, smiling tenderly.

"You have already given me a life. What more could you possibly have to give me?" she said, her voice strained with emotion and wonder.

"Freedom." He said.

Her head snapped back in shock and surprise. What does He mean? He had already set her free from so much...she couldn't fathom the possibility of more.

"Freedom?" she asked tremulously.

"If you will let me walk with you, you can be free from the pain of the past and any pain that will find you in the future. In this life you will always have suffering, but a purpose and a meaning can come and what was meant to harm you can be used for good to help others. Will you let me walk with you in the pain of that past so that you can be free to endure the future?" his eyes examined her piercingly, but also lovingly.

Meg grew uneasy again as she began to hear her mother's hurtful words and horrible names that she had frequently called her. Then she heard a list of things that she had herself done and froze, horrified. Where was this coming from? As far as she knew no one else knew the evil she had perpetrated in her heart, or acted out in her deeds! She looked around to find the source of the disembodied voice, and found it in an impish creature sitting on a box and shrieking the assaults in her direction.

"Stop it! He will hear and know I'm trash!" she screamed in her thoughts. She closed her eyes and shook her head and let the tears flow down her cheeks.

"You can do this. You can make him stop. Will you let me walk with you?"

She looked around and was overwhelmed by the number and size of the boxes. She knew what was in them. She was sure she couldn't face it, any of it. She was struggling because she knew

168

she would disappoint him with the contents and number of her sins contained within them, but she was sure she didn't have the strength. She looked up again and knew she must find the strength, for the love in his eyes was so tender and unquestioning that she couldn't bear to fail him. He had given her so much already; she could give him this.

She gripped his hands tighter and nodded her head in assent. With that he turned to the imp and without a word the imp went screaming and screeching into the shadows as if burned by fire. Meg jumped at the noise and at the fact that box was now tipping towards her, it's lid thrown off. Meg steeled herself and held on to Him tighter because she knew what was in there.

"This is bad, this is bad, this is so bad!!" she shouted in her head.

The box hit the ground with a thud, and Meg watched in horror as the contents fell out into the pool of light in the center of the floor.

Meg stared…and stared…not comprehending what she was seeing. The object was much, much smaller than the box; less than a tenth in size. She stared at the thing, confused.

"There is something you need to understand here, Meg; your fear of facing this thing created the box around it. The bigger the fear, the bigger the box. You have a tendency to build big boxes around some small things because you have lived in fear for so long. Let's look." He said as he moved her closer to object.

Meg held tighter to his hands and took small, tentative steps towards the familiar object. As they reached it, Meg stood over it in the light and marveled at it.

"Is that all you are?" She said. "I can't believe that's all you are." It was at that moment that she learned to drag things that were painful kicking and screaming into the light so that the truth could be known. It was the unknown and the secrets in the darkness that held her captive and she was finally choosing not to hold herself hostage to the boxes in the darkness.

Over those two years the Lord visited her frequently in dreams, and they went through all of the boxes together. Most of them were the right sized boxes for the things they contained. She would cling to the truth that He was revealing to her through each encounter. He was more real to her than almost anything else in her world. He was healing her as she painfully and patiently continued to open boxes and deal with what was in them. She gained insight and perspective on the most painful events of her life. She found forgiveness for herself and for those who had violated her. She found that the more she processed and the more she worked, the fewer and fewer nightmares and flashbacks she would have. She began to grow real attachments, and found parts of herself awakening from what felt like a long, extinguishing slumber. She found compassion and she found concern for others and perhaps most importantly, she began to trust; in herself, in the Lord, in her husband and children and even in strangers.

He continued to help her until the very last box had been opened. He told her he would not be far from her, and that there were things she was going to do and that he would come to her again soon; but for now, she should walk in liberty with her family and enjoy the freedom. It was a bittersweet goodbye. She had never known or been shown such love and she knew he would always be there all the way every day.

CHAPTER 26

TRAINING

O ver the next few years Meg and her little family grew in the Lord and understanding. She never let go of her pursuit of Jesus' presence in her life and sought diligently to become the person she could be in His eyes. Her children also grew.

At one point the Lord came to her and told her it was time to find a church. She had devoured the Word of the Lord and the Holy Spirit had been active in teaching her and her encounters with the Lord had catapulted her to a place of truth and light. She was no longer plagued with the nightmares and flashbacks, she was fully awake and alive and engaged in everyday life with her family. She was *happy*!

She had made great strides forward in maturing and understanding, managing the pain in life along with the pleasure. She had physical struggles within her body that had plagued her from the time she was 18 resulting in infertility, weight gain and mood swings. She had had 5 miscarriages since her son was born. She had sought help from doctors, only to be told repeatedly that she was fat and needed to stop eating and exercise more. She knew there was something more wrong with her, because the truth was that she hardly ate anything. She finally got a doctor to listen when she taped a program from a TV news documentary. She took the tape to a new doctor and pleaded with him to watch the tape and see if he could get her in the study that was being done by a doctor in Chicago. Her new doctor watched the tape conferred with the doctor in Chicago and Meg was ecstatic to learn that she indeed now had a proper diagnosis. The study was closed, but her doctor received information and instructions for treatment and medication for her condition which he prescribed right away. Within a three months the weight was coming off and the other symptoms were beginning to abate. She thanked God for the whole set of circumstances that came together to make it all work. Through this trial she had learned from the Lord that she was battling from a place of victory because though He had already won it for her, she still had to continue through the process and find Him and His purpose in it.

The doctor actually thanked her for her persistence in pursuing an answer. He said that he knew it mustn't have been easy for her because before her he had no answer for women with her condition except to treat the infertility. He said that he felt he could now help more women like her, whereas before he wouldn't have been able to. Meg didn't know what to do with that.

Something began to form in her around the experiences. She had been volunteering and started food distribution programs in the church and worked at a local homeless shelter as well but found it to be less of an answer than a band aid. There were so many limitations and restrictions to actually helping people that the results were minimal.

She had been so excited when she learned that she was going to go to church. She was finally going to be part of the larger family of Christ and have a place to be supported and to support others. She was going to find a place to serve God and be part of the body in His house. She was going to learn more and worship Him with other believers. How wonderful would that be!

Her example of the disciples in the bible was part of her hunger to be part of the larger body. They worked together leading others to Christ and raising them up to pursue others as well. They were all part of the same team and though there were some rough patches, the pursuit of Christ and His mission were always paramount.

Jesus said "You will know who are mine by the way they love one another."

She wanted to be a part of that. Love had not just awakened in her, it erupted out of her everywhere she went! She paid for the groceries of those in line behind her because they looked like they were having difficulty, even though she couldn't afford it herself; but God always provided and made it up so they always had what they needed (*wanted* was another matter, of course).

The first Sunday she went to a church she came away disappointed. It had been a very sterile experience. It was the same denomination that her husband had attended in childhood. She thought, "No wonder he didn't know the Jesus guy." It was mostly form and ritual and a lot of standing up and down and repeating stuff and a very dry sermon and then repeating of the Apostles Creed and then out to lunch. No one really welcomed them or acknowledged them. She did hear some ladies talking about them while she was in the bathroom stall. They were very unkind about how she was dressed and that they couldn't believe she would wear pants to church or bring her children into church dressed that way either. She waited in the stall until she was sure they were gone. After they left she told her husband when they were at home that they needed to keep looking and told him of her encounter. He said it was just like he remembered; even the gossipy unkind women. He agreed they needed to keep looking.

The little family visited several different churches yet found the same kinds of people. Some had the ritualistic style that she didn't care for and others were middle of the road vanilla and

a few downright scared them with their people running up and down the aisles barking or laughing hysterically. Every week she would go back to the Word and see what she was missing because none of what she was experiencing or seeing was what she saw in the book. Was she just not comprehending properly? She had gone in search of Ephesus and continuously found Corinth.

When the Holy Spirit finally seated them in what she thought was the right congregation it was a whirlwind of experiences and feelings. The church was far from perfect, but had most of what she felt was kindred to her spirit. She threw herself in one hundred percent, and started the pursuit of Christ as a member of a body. Her excitement was short lived. She didn't realize that inside the walls there were cultural constraints and that you had to earn acceptance and that there was a hierarchy amongst the people from the pulpit to the pew and that the ultimate goal was dominance.

She learned all of this the hard way. She would cry out to the Lord and ask what she had done wrong when she thought she was just doing what the great commission had outlined, and the "enforcers" would come and constrain her. Her relationship with the Pastor was great; it was her relating with her fellow congregants that was the problem.

She stood up from her task of mopping the floor and laughed a little. Her fatal mistake all those years ago had been the same as Joseph's. She had gone to the brethren and told them of her visitations with the Lord and they ate her alive.

She didn't understand at the time what was wrong until she came to the realization that a visitation from the Lord was not a common experience among Christians apparently. She had only her own experience and the accounts from the bible to draw from so she didn't know it was considered to be rare, and that *if* the Lord was going to visit someone it wouldn't be the likes of her. She had also made the mistake of telling them her past and apparently being a teenage out of wedlock mother even though you married later was a less than desirable asset to the congregation. There were those who would use it against her when it came time for positions or promotions in the church. Meg had never pursued a position or promotion. She did anything and everything she could to fill in and help anyone. She would wash dishes happily because she was grateful to do anything in the House of the Lord. She would be asked to do a task and she would do it to the best of her ability as if unto the Lord. She took every class offered and was there for every event usually in a help capacity.

In every instance when someone would talk to her about why they didn't like what she was doing or that she needed correction from it they would always say "It's just your personality. People can't handle the way you are and you need to change how you are with them. It's partly because you're a woman and some people feel you are intimidating and too strong." Again she knew she wasn't perfect and she was changing, but these things....how could she change her personality or her gender? She would try harder and do better. Unfortunately it seemed there was no pleasing them, and she would not lose herself so shortly after finding it. She always seemed to find out about the gossip or the problems after they happened; how could she always be the last to know about issues that revolved around her? She couldn't understand why there was any attention paid to her at all let alone this vicious stuff. She thought she must be doing something to make so many people angry with her.

Her next mistake was going to three church ladies to talk about the issues. After all, the book said that if you know of someone that has aught with you, you were to go to them and work it out and she wanted to do things properly. Meg approached them in an apologetic manner asking them what she had done and how she could make it right. They were haughty and arrogant toward her and she felt like she was trash. They spoke to her about how highly she must think of herself to think that they would even concern themselves with her.

She wondered if she had been given wrong information and berated herself for listening to gossip. She apologized again and went before the Lord. It was a large struggle for her. Then she learned it was all true when the same ladies and some men in the congregation mounted a coup against the Pastor. The resulting split devastated her. How could this be happening in God's house? Didn't we all profess to believe in the same Jesus and live by the same book? Mistrust and abuse were back in her life uninvited. An interim Pastor was brought in and he was there for several months before another Pastor entered the congregation.

After she had met him she had had high hopes that he could re-unite or at least unify the broken pieces that were left and rebuild. The Lord had shown her in the book where this had happened over and over again among his people when they lacked focus and vision from Him and pursued their own agendas. Unfortunately everyone pays a price for their pride. The three women had left shortly after the interim Pastor had arrived and Meg never knew why nor did she pursue an answer. The small group that was left was able to unify under the leadership of the new Pastor.

Meg had been called in shortly after the new Pastor had arrived. She had been asked to help out with the office while the secretary was on vacation on the day the new Pastor came in. One of the Elders in the congregation didn't care for her and she knew it because he had made it known to her personally. She at least respected that he came to her but was unable to change his mind about her as he felt she had an agenda and a spirit of control and on and on and on. Meg asked God to search her heart and let her know if this were true. She knew that she was doing whatever was asked of her and she was not pursuing her own power or position. She was trying to help keep the ship upright with those who were left by doing what was asked without seeking any type of reward.

The day the new Pastor arrived an Elder was supposed to be there to give him the keys and take him to the parsonage and help him settle in. Instead, the wife of the Elder called the church where Meg was volunteering in the office, and asked her to take the key to the parsonage over to the new Pastor, who would meet her there.

Meg did as she was asked and met the Pastor at the parsonage and delivered the key and showed him around and asked if there was anything else she could do or any questions he had etc. She had been told that the Elder would be arriving at a certain time and had told the Pastor this and asked him if it was ok if she got back to the church, as it was unattended in her absence. He thanked her for her help and she went back to the church office.

Shortly after arriving back at her desk the phone rang. She answered it in a pleasant voice and was greeted by the Overseer who was obviously upset with her. She listened as he outlined her high crimes and misdemeanors of the afternoon. He stated that he had received a call from the Elder who disliked her and that he stated that she put herself in the position of getting to the Pastor by taking the key to him at the parsonage and pushing her own agenda to be in control. He asked if she knew that the other Elder was assigned the task of meeting the pastor with the key and without waiting for an answer he began to correct her accursedly controlling and arrogant ways based on the information he had received from the Elder. He told her that she needed to close the office and go home and that they would get someone else to fill in for the secretary. This was too much. The all too familiar hot tears of shame and embarrassment began to flow down her cheeks. What was wrong with her that people thought they could talk to her in such a way? Was she never going to be allowed to answer her accusers or defend herself?

"Are you crying?" the Overseer asked.

She couldn't answer at first. She sniffed and took a deep breath because now she was mad. "Not because I did what you said but because I am accused, tried and executed without being allowed to explain what really happened and that was not supposed to happen to me among the Lord's people. I am locking up and going home like you told me to but you need to call the other Elder and find the truth in the situation. Maybe I'm not the one who needs correction this time. Goodbye."

She drove home crying and wondering if she would ever be able to exist around other people without drawing conflict. What was she supposed to do to change her personality? How could she make people feel not intimidated by her? What was she doing that made them feel that way anyway? She was the common denominator in all of the conflicts after all. She knew she needed to work on herself but didn't feel she had any positive example of what she was supposed to look like. She really, truly was trying.

When she got home there was a message asking her to call the Elder who had tattled on her. She truly didn't want to speak to him and listen to another ten reasons why he felt she shouldn't be allowed to breathe or exist in the body. She steeled herself and told herself that if anything redemptive was ever going to come out of this then she needed to endure and allow the Lord to work on her.

She called the number and the Elder answered. She said, "I have a message that you wanted to speak with me."

"Yeah...ummm...yeah...I guess I need to apologize. I, uh, I didn't know that James' wife called you and asked you to drop off the key. I just assumed with your history that you did it without permission. So I uh am sorry."

Meg was stunned. "I'm sorry, what was that about my history of not having permission? What are you talking about? I have never done anything without permission or been asked to do? I don't understand!"

"Look, we all know that you want to be out front and that you have to be in the center of everything. You have your fingers in everything and you are controlling. We are praying that God will teach you humility and that you will repent."

Again Meg was stunned. This is how they interpreted her service and her motivation? This was the consensus?

"That is what you truly believe, isn't it. You truly believe that I am deliberately trying to seek power and position?" she said. She heard her own voice. It was confident and strong. She was finally standing up for herself. She would no longer apologize for someone else's interpretation of who she was in her soul or actions. None of them had taken the time to truly get to know her. They judged and they acted on that judgment without wisdom or truth. The Book talked about this too. She was so glad that she knew the Book and the One of whom it proclaimed.

"We have seen your kind before and had to deal with them too." He said, tersely.

"I thank you for calling and letting me know that the misunderstanding was figured out. I hope you have a good week." She said as pleasantly as she could.

She went before the Lord. She prayed that He would release her from this congregation and let her find another. He would not. She had to stay. Over the next year the woman was forced to sit and prove her obedience. She was told that she could attend but that she was not allowed to hold a position or do anything without permission.

Outwardly the woman was pleasant and acted as if all was well. Inwardly, she was struggling. She heard other women saying nasty things about her. She began to feel as she did in school when her brothers would humiliate her in public. These women were more practiced at their stealth. Their gossip remained in tight circles in which Meg seemed to forever remain on the periphery. Meg felt defeated and hopeless but the Lord would encourage her as she prayed.

She read in the book that others had gone through similar and worse things as her, and found her strength within their own. She found the Lord to be faithful to her and present with her. Every week Meg would attend Church faithfully, and sat in her designated area and worshipped the Lord with all that was within her. She was very open in her worship. She sang and moved freely, not caring what she looked like or who saw her. It wasn't for them anyway; it was to Her Lord that she sang.

She began to draw away from the church and pursue some education and became an EMT. While she was in school she began to feel restless and insecure. She felt as if she weren't doing enough for the Lord.

On the night of her Finals she was driving the thirty miles to class. She had been listening to a teaching tape by a Pastor who talked about pursuing God and the fruit that should be seen in a true Christian's life. Meg felt small and pathetic. She was failing Him! She wasn't doing anything for Him and He must be so disappointed in her. She had truly tried to do good! She had only ended up in detention again like in school. No matter what she did it wasn't going to be right. He must be so disappointed in her!

The next thing she knew, She was in this brightly lit space and...no...it couldn't be....it was! The Lord was standing before her beckoning her to come to Him. Her heart leapt at the sight of Him with His outstretched hands waiting for hers to fill them. She hesitated, confused. Was He not going to chastise her? Was He going to show her His disapproval and disappointment? She flushed and looked at the floor and forced her feet to move toward Him. She would take whatever He was going to say and do. She made it to Him and looked at His still outstretched hands. She couldn't take His in hers. She wasn't righteous. She wasn't pure.

She had failed again and been ostracized, made to sit for bad behavior. She couldn't look at Him knowing she was such a pain.

He reached out and took her hand in one of His and with the other He lifted her chin to look at Him.

"Daughter!" He said smiling.

What is this? She thought. *He shouldn't be happy to see me right now!*

"Daughter, do you know why these people are here?" He said looking intently into her eyes with such kindness and love.

It was at that point that she noticed all of the people singing and dancing around a table with an abundance of food and drink. How could she have missed them?

She looked longingly at them as they freely danced and sang and ate together. What was it like to be that free?

"They are here because you are the King and they worship you!" she said in a tiny voice.

"No, Daughter. Look at me."

She looked Him full in the face with hot tears streaming down her cheeks, ashamed and weary. His eyes locked her gaze with a force she had never known and she couldn't have looked away even if she had wanted to.

"They are dancing and singing and rejoicing because they are happy to see you - and so am I!" He brushed His fingers gently across her cheek.

"Dance with me, Daughter." He pulled her in close to Him and danced with her. Here she felt complete. Here it made sense. Here she could see Him and feel Him and know Him without anything in the way. She clung to Him tightly.

"I'm so sorry Lord! I didn't mean to make another mess. I don't know what I'm doing and why I am always doing the wrong thing!" she said breathlessly and miserably. She was trying hard not to sob like a baby.

"Why do you think you are to blame?" He asked as He whirled her around the room.

"Because the Pastor made me sit and told me that I had to learn obedience. He had said that I was always going to have trouble because my light shines too bright. I don't even know what that means!"

Jesus chuckled for a moment but then became very serious. He lifted her chin up so she would look at Him again.

"You are not to blame for what others think of you. You are not defined by their words, actions or deeds. You are who I say you are. I say you are a daughter born of Almighty God and are highly valued and precious to me. I say you are loved and cherished and worth more than any pearl or price to be paid. You will conquer giants and you will battle for those who are not strong enough to battle for themselves. You are my beloved. Dance with me a little longer....until you believe it for yourself."

Everything in her wanted to believe what He was saying. Her heart was screaming, "But Lord, I screwed up again and I don't even know how or what I did!" The longer she danced with Him the less she felt the need to think or talk about her unworthiness. She felt safe here with Him.

She never wanted to leave.

PART 3
AT THE PEAK

CHAPTER 27

FAITHFUL GOD

Meg sat at her desk in her new beautiful office. She stared around the room at the décor and marveled at her blessings!

On the far wall hung the many gifts given to her from her various students that she had taught over the years. It had been ten years! She couldn't believe it! A lot had happened!

"Lord, I am truly, truly grateful. You have been my Savior and Lord, my friend and the lover of my soul. You have given far more than silver or gold. You have given me life. Thank you." She closed her eyes and said the words out loud and in her spirit with all she had she kissed toward the Lord with love and gratitude.

"We aren't done yet!" He said laughing. "There's more, remember?"

Her eyes flew open and, lo and behold, He was there with her. His eyes danced with love and - what was this - was it actually mischief?

"It is good to see you my Lord! Look at what your people have done! This place has been restored as a testimony to your goodness and to your purposes. We are so grateful to be given favor among our community. They see you in what we are trying to do.

I hope you are pleased, Lord." She said, smiling at Him with glee in her eyes and her heart.

"I am pleased." He said, smiling back.

Her heart leapt in her chest. Oh to hear those words from Him, here in this place! She was ecstatic. His people had been so generous and faithful and committed to restoring this building to house His purposes and those trapped in addiction and others who would recover here and those who would learn here and go out from here to be His hands extended to heal.

Tonight was the dedication, so there was a lot of activity going on. None of that chaos and hubbub registered at this moment. He was here. She stared and took in the sight of Him. His eyes shone and danced with love and pleasure, like a parent looking at their child, playing with a gift just opened.

"Lord, what can I do for you? Is there something I need to do?" she asked expectantly.

"I have come to give you something. It is for this time and place. Tonight when you pray with my people tell them this: See, I have set you at the gates of this city. No one will be able to enter or leave without going through your prayers. It is a beginning. Be faithful and watch and pray. You will do great things and have favor with men and with me." He touched her cheek with those last words. "Beloved, well done."

The tears flowed down her cheeks at His words and at His countenance with her. She couldn't believe He could feel this way about her! Yes, she and the others worked hard to get here but she had made a lot of mistakes along the way! It was all covered in wonderful and awful. Blood, sweat and tears birthed this place; hers and those of many others, too.

"Lord, the others here, they love you so much and are willing to sacrifice and serve you and your people and purposes. We are just trying to do what you want us to do. I cannot get a well done without them. *They* built this for you it wasn't just me." Her face was crimson with embarrassment that He should utter those two words to her. She was not worthy of it, she was only one of many who loved Him here.

He laughed out loud and the sound was so rich in timbre that it vibrated in her chest. She looked up through her tear clouded eyes and saw the delight in His.

He picked her up and hugged her and she squealed in surprise. "I must go, and you have much to do. Remember to tell them what I said." His face became serious as He said the words. "There are dark days ahead Meg, and I need you strong. Dig deeper and equip them to better hear me themselves. My sheep know my voice…but then again they don't. Teach them and make them my disciples. Love them well and lead them on to me. Keep your armor on and remember my provision and promises. You have more giants to conquer. " With that He was gone.

That night more than a hundred people came to the dedication. There were speeches and tours and exclamations of surprise at the grandeur that had been born from a derelict building. It had been in such a state of disrepair that it had been scheduled to be torn down. Now it had been restored and made beautiful and dedicated to the Lord and His purposes.

After the guests left, Meg stood in the midst of God's faithful people. They had built this place right alongside her as He had provided for it.

She began to speak. She told them of her gratitude for them and that the Lord was pleased. She told them what He had told her. That He has set them at the gate of this city and that no one would be able to come in or out without being touched by the prayers from here. She began to pray and they prayed with her in gratitude and faith and with thanksgiving. His glory filled the room. His presence was thick and tangible among His people as she declared that this place would be known as a habitation of the Lord, as a place where the presence of the Lord dwells, and a place of peace and rest. And it is.

"What is man that you are mindful of him and the Son of man that you visit him?" And He does.

"Love the Lord your God with all your heart, with all your mind and with all your strength." And I do.

22385298R00126

Made in the USA
Middletown, DE
28 July 2015